transforming
disruption
to **impact**

www.amplifypublishing.com

Transforming Disruption to Impact:
Rethinking Volunteer Engagement for a Rapidly Changing World

For more information, please contact:
Amplify Publishing, an imprint of Amplify Publishing Group
620 Herndon Parkway, Suite 320
Herndon, VA 20170
info@amplifypublishing.com

Library of Congress Control Number: 2021925398

CPSIA Code: PRV0522A

ISBN-13: 978-1-63755-286-5

Printed in the United States

To all the innovative and brave leaders who saw volunteers as valued partners even amid disruptions, and to those whose stories are in these pages and the many others whose stories are unfolding in communities around the world. Thank you for your inspiration and for transforming the future of engagement.

transforming disruption to impact

Rethinking Volunteer Engagement for a Rapidly Changing World

EDITED BY

Doug Bolton   **Beth Steinhorn**
Jerome Tennille   **Craig Young**

an imprint of Amplify Publishing Group

Contents

Introduction
Transforming Disruption to Impact

Parents organizing a fundraiser for their child's swim team.

Entrepreneurs serving on an organization's social enterprise committee.

Teenagers shoveling the driveway of an older neighbor.

Interpreters guiding a class of students around a sculpture garden.

These are just a few of the many images that comprise the intricate tapestry of volunteerism that society has woven over the last century. But events in 2020 transformed that fabric—completely unraveling some sections, fraying other areas, and adding entirely new threads throughout.

Due to safety concerns and government restrictions in response to the COVID-19 pandemic, nearly every sector involving volunteers (including those in private industry, governmental, faith-based, and nonprofit organizations) was affected. Many of these organizations shut down volunteer activities entirely, while others adapted existing volunteer practices or engaged an unprecedented number of volunteers to meet an extraordinary increase in demand for services. Others engaged volunteers in completely new ways. For most organizations, COVID-19 disrupted volunteering at all levels.

Volunteer engagement—when leveraged effectively—is a strategy that builds an organization's capacity to accomplish its mission. Whether committed to reducing food insecurity, protecting wildlife, educating the public on economic policy, or enhancing life through the arts, organizations that harness volunteer talent can increase mission-driven impact. The pandemic disrupted not only volunteering, but also the extent to which organizations could tap into this mission-critical strategy.

Disruption is challenging. For organizational leaders, volunteers, and the communities being served, the interruption and limitations were naturally disheartening, disturbing, and disconcerting. Yet, *disruption is not inherently bad*. Disruption can be the impetus to release ourselves from the tyranny of "the way we've always done things." If viewed as an opportunity, disruption invites us to revisit, rethink, and reinvent the way we achieve our mission. It may even prompt us to retire practices that no longer serve us. In short, disruption can bring about new perspective.

New perspectives are not limited to finding ways to engage volunteers virtually or reducing numbers of volunteers serving at any one time to mitigate the spread of the virus. The disruptions associated with the pandemic are compounded by a marked increase in awareness of racial inequities. The convergence of these crises is no coincidence. The pandemic revealed cracks and stressors that have long existed in society—and, in doing so, exposed the inequities within volunteer engagement, funding, and nonprofits in general. Lack of racial, ethnic, economic, and age diversity within many volunteer forces, limited access to technology, and lack of digital literacy are all fractures in the foundation which have become more apparent and even widened amid the COVID-19 crisis.

Research prior to the pandemic showed a positive correlation between effective volunteer engagement and an organization's ability to be more adaptable, sustainable, and scalable.[*] Throughout the pandemic and its associated economic crisis, this finding was reinforced; the organizations that leveraged volunteer engagement as a strategy to respond to the pandemic are the same organizations that are surviving—if not thriving—despite it.

The pandemic is nothing to celebrate. Nevertheless, the leaders of these organizations recognized the opportunity in the crisis and effectively transformed disruption into impact. As a society, the pandemic's ripple effects continue—with economic fallout that will be felt for years. While many organizations are shifting from response to reopening, that does not mean we should return to the ways we did business prior to the pandemic.

As we continue to weather disruptions and begin to rebuild, we have a choice: Reopen with the programs, services, and volunteer practices that were in place prior to the pandemic or to build back better. We now have the opportunity to reengineer how we tap volunteer talent and contributions so that we,

---

[*] TCC Group, "National Core Capacity Assessment Tool Dataset: Positive Deviants in Volunteerism and Service," December 2009, https://s3.amazonaws.com/pol-website/media/reimaginingservice/u2/TCC%20Group%20Positive%20Deviant%20Research.pdf.

too, transform disruption into impact. We have case studies, models, and successes upon which to build. We can learn from those who have already turned disruption into impact. We can apply their lessons to our work and leverage volunteers as partners to position our organizations and communities for adaptability, sustainability, and scalability, regardless of what the future brings. We can strengthen our transformational muscles so that we can convert these disruptions into mission-critical impact fueled by strategic volunteer engagement.

This book offers a collection of proven pathways to impact. The collected contributions feature accounts of organizations that chose innovation in response to disruption. These organizations, in the heat of crisis, chose to reexamine the landscape of volunteering to identify the opportunities rather than lament the challenges. They chose to rethink strategies around how volunteers could still drive mission fulfillment, rethink engagement by accelerating practices that may have existed prior to the pandemic but quickly became more vital to success, and even rethink how the impact of volunteer involvement is tracked, measured, communicated, and celebrated.

- **Section One** lays out the foundation for rethinking the landscape of volunteering during the pandemic, economic crisis, and evolving generations. It also casts a brighter spotlight on racial inequities and injustices.
- **Section Two** challenges us to rethink strategy, including volunteering and civic engagement, the relationship between philanthropy and volunteering, corporate volunteering, and the role of executive leadership.

- **Section Three** inspires us to rethink the fundamental practices of engagement, including recruitment and technology, mentoring, and designated days of service.
- **Section Four** explores the end result of the transformation: impact. It addresses capturing impact, leveraging national service to increase impact, and amplifying impact through strategic investments.

Throughout the sections, common themes emerge. Since the inception of the pandemic, virtual volunteering has certainly taken center stage. While not a novel concept—many organizations began engaging volunteers in virtual service over three decades ago—the urgency posed by recent events finally knocked down the remaining walls of resistance still held by some staff members. Those who had been reluctant to engage volunteers virtually due to lack of trust or ability to rely on in-person oversight finally recognized that volunteers could serve responsibly and effectively—and be held accountable—even if not sitting in a nearby cubicle. As companies and organizations were forced to allow employees to work remotely, those same employees and leaders were finally able to imagine engaging and supporting volunteers working remotely as well. While virtual volunteering is not an innovation in and of itself, it is a thread throughout many of these stories because it is, in fact, a practice that made innovation possible.

Similarly, developing new services to address unprecedented and changing community needs, recognizing the potential to connect with informally organized volunteer networks, and prioritizing a sense of community that extends beyond in-person events and celebrations are woven throughout many stories that follow.

Rebuilding is a never-ending journey and will require a commitment to growth, change, and adaptability. But now is the time to point our compasses toward impactful engagement and start mapping out the path in that direction. We have gathered these stories and insights to serve as signposts along the journey, but they alone are not the sum of the stories or data to guide us.

This collection is but a signpost offering diverse pathways to the future. As you break the trail of your own journey from disruption to impact, we encourage you to share, learn, and discuss, as you will be authoring your own innovations and adaptations from which others can learn and take inspiration. Then, we can move forward together, from disruption to impact, fueled by the most abundant resource of all: volunteer power.

So let our journey begin.

Doug Bolton
Beth Steinhorn
Jerome Tennille
Craig Young

Landscape of Disruption

Time of Crisis: Leadership for Volunteering and Community Resilience

Nichole Cirillo and Wendy Osborne

Nichole Cirillo joined International Association for Volunteer Effort (IAVE) as Executive Director in October 2019. She believes in the power of volunteers to change the world and sees IAVE as an activator and thought leadership organization helping to both support volunteering globally and advance the conversation and understanding on the importance of volunteering and volunteering leadership. Nichole has significant executive experience across environmental and social justice sectors and has led the engagement of a large network of global volunteers. Her roles have included Mission Director/Head of PR at Stonyfield Organics, International Director of Learning at Earthwatch, Senior Manager, Outreach and Mobilization at Unitarian Universalist Service Committee (UUSC) and Executive Director at Friends of the Public Garden and Boston Common.

Wendy Osborne, OBE, retired as Chief Executive of Volunteer Now in Northern Ireland, United Kingdom (UK), in 2017. She has over thirty-five years of experience working in the field of volunteer support and development. She has provided leadership locally, nationally, and internationally and has substantive experience with influencing and developing national policies for volunteering at a Northern Ireland and UK level. In 2001 she was awarded the Officer of the Order of the British Empire (OBE) by Her Majesty the Queen for services to volunteering. She has recently been working as a Senior Consultant to IAVE on a range of projects including their global convenings and research and development work with national leadership for volunteering organizations.

* * *

The Peruvian experience—"'Intense, exhausting and heartbreaking,' says a forty-one-year-old volunteer when asked how she would describe her work. She drives daily throughout Lima, delivering food and water to the poorest families in order to help them get through the quarantine."*

The African experience—"Fear started gripping Africa. One of the biggest concerns was the inadequate health care systems throughout the continent. With all the fears, rising numbers of confirmed cases, and reported deaths, volunteers demonstrated extreme selfless acts of care. The kind of resilience exhibited by volunteers and volunteer-involving organizations was immense. In the spirit of 'stronger together,'

---

* Vanessa Vasquez et al., "Together we take charge," *IAVE Volunteering Together Magazine*, no. 7 (May 2020): https://www.iave.org/volunteering-together-magazine/issue-7/.

the focus has gradually shifted (during 2021) to post coronavirus. What will the world look like? What were some of the lessons learned? What can be done now to prepare us for future scenarios?'"*

The sentiments behind these quotes represent an almost universal experience to COVID-19. Countries and communities were faced with a massive threat to human life, and the response to contain the spread of the virus and protect lives, however necessary, also threatened livelihoods, disrupted social networks, and brought about forced isolation.

In the face of this global disaster, volunteer-involving organizations and community-led volunteering became a vital part—and sometimes the only part—of the emergency response while continuing to meet existing community needs.

Breaking Point

The pandemic changed the way we live our lives, creating fear, uncertainty, instability, a lack of momentum, and a sense of isolation. These same issues also affected the volunteering community, including national volunteering leadership organizations.† The International Association for Volunteer Effort

---

* Fred Sadia, "Africa rising up in solidarity," *IAVE Volunteering Together Magazine*, no. 9 (May 2021): https://www.iave.org/volunteering-together-magazine/issue-9/volunteering-together-issue-9/.

† IAVE describes national volunteering leadership organizations as "operating at a national level or a strategic regional level to promote and support volunteering, having linkages and/or active relationships/partnerships with volunteer-involving organizations, government, and corporations, as well as institutions such as United Nations Volunteers when appropriate."

(IAVE)* believes that national leadership for volunteering organizations raises awareness of the strategic value of volunteering, gets more people involved as volunteers, and develops and builds capacity to enhance the effectiveness and impact of the volunteers' contributions. These organizations have active linkages and partnerships with governments, corporations and institutions, and any number of local organizations in the communities they serve. This enhances volunteer practice and harnesses the power for collective action at the local and societal level. This, in turn, supports the development of an enabling environment that builds resilient communities—the kind of communities that can deal with crisis by either averting the breaking point or rebounding effectively.

In responding to the pandemic, evidence† shows that national volunteering leadership organizations faced significant challenges. In some countries, it was challenging to gain recognition for the important contribution volunteers could make during the crisis. The mobilization of volunteers was necessary to provide help during the pandemic, but the challenge of keeping volunteers safe was also of paramount importance.

During lockdowns, face-to-face volunteering was difficult if not impossible. Huge numbers of volunteers were within an age bracket that made them more vulnerable to the virus, which meant they were no longer available to volunteer. Supporting volunteer-involving organizations in effective volunteer

---

*   IAVE—the International Association for Volunteer Effort—is a 501(c)(3) organization whose mission is to create a more just and sustainable world by enabling leaders, leadership organizations and environments that empower volunteers. www.iave.org.

†   Jacob Mwathi et al., "Leadership for Volunteering: the COVID-19 Experience," A research study for IAVE, 2021, https://leadership4vol.iave.org.

engagement was also challenging, as capacity-building activities became impossible to continue because most of this required face-to-face engagement. There were also issues of supply and demand within some countries, with many individuals signing up to volunteer and not enough formal opportunities available.

While in other countries, the withdrawal of older people from volunteering due to health reasons left a huge gap for organizations to fulfill demands for help. Many countries in the global North experienced an emergence of informal volunteering at the community level that challenged how community-led activism could work effectively alongside organizations that involve volunteers in a more formal process of engagement. Countries in the global South saw a rise in community-led volunteering as the deployment of international volunteers decreased due to safety issues and travel restrictions associated with COVID-19. This all caused disruption for volunteering on a substantive scale.

"In any moment of decision, the best thing you can do is the right thing, the next best thing is the wrong thing, and the worst thing you can do is nothing."* Several leadership for volunteering organizations have indicated that, at the beginning of the pandemic, there was inertia caused by the speed of change and the uncertainty of what to do in response. However, the IAVE research report "Leadership for Volunteering: The COVID-19 Experience"† identifies clearly that organizations were adaptive and became adept at finding solutions to the volunteering challenges posed by COVID-19.

---

*   A statement often attributed to Theodore Roosevelt, twenty-sixth U.S. President.

†   Jacob Mwathi et al., "Leadership for Volunteering."

"Within crisis are the seeds of opportunity."* The previously referenced IAVE research study examines how COVID-19 impacted the strategic role of leadership for volunteering organizations in advocacy, development, and volunteer mobilization. It collected data from seventy organizations across sixty-seven countries. It is clear from the research that the pandemic increased the complexity of the volunteering environment; it created challenges for volunteering, yet also created opportunities for development and innovation.

Disruptive Innovation

Key findings from the research indicate that in the context of the pandemic, the increased use and development of technology have been key factors. The national volunteering leadership organizations created portals and websites to help manage the supply and demand for volunteering. They developed more online opportunities and quickly adjusted their communication and support for volunteering to virtual.

An example is the Israeli Volunteering Council, which designed new virtual volunteering roles that could be carried out from the volunteer's home. The council supported volunteer managers in creating new roles and tasks, along with providing the necessary training to enable volunteers to carry out these new roles with confidence. For many organizations, moving to more online activity was a necessity. This notable change also had to be thoroughly resourced and managed. It is equally important to note that the world has many digital

---

* A statement often attributed to Marilyn Monroe, American actress, model, and singer.

divides, across continents and within countries. Using and maximizing technology as a resource presented a challenge for organizations where consistent, affordable connectivity is a problem.

Another key finding of the research concerns the importance of partnerships and coalitions. In several countries, national leadership for volunteering organizations strengthened their volunteer-based partnerships with government. New coalitions with volunteer-involving organizations have also been developed to support volunteer mobilization.

While volunteering activity has both increased and decreased at different times and in different countries during this pandemic period, the report's findings indicate that organizations engaged a wider diversity of volunteers and that most of the national leadership for volunteering organizations see inclusivity as a key feature of future volunteer mobilization strategies.

The following examples highlight in more detail some of the pandemic-induced challenges faced by two leadership for volunteering organizations, and the innovative solutions that were developed. The examples are linked to one or more of the five elements of resilient communities as set out by Benjamin J. Lough, PhD, University of Illinois.[*]

- **Connected communities** with robust social networks and active partnerships.
- **Participatory communities** where people feel empowered, self-organize, and display organic leadership.

[*] Benjamin Lough, "The Thread that Binds: Volunteering and Community Resilience," Literature Review for the State of the World's Volunteerism Report, 2017: https://doi.org/10.18356/14b33d1a-en.

- **Socially cohesive communities** where you see solidarity, shared values, and people working well together.
- **Able-to-learn communities** with strong systems in place for information and regulatory feedback.
- **Diverse communities** where members have different and complementary qualities.*

Mobilizing Volunteers in Hong Kong (AVS Hong Kong)

In Hong Kong, the key challenges were social isolation with already vulnerable people, such as the elderly, being made ever more vulnerable through the disruption of existing social networks and a shortage of safety items such as masks. The initial lack of a coordinated response created a duplication of resources that resulted in ineffective service delivery to meet emerging needs.

The key strategies that worked to address these issues included a focus on planning, advocacy, and mobilizing volunteers safely. Responding quickly to the emerging situation, including rolling out a volunteer recruitment program within a single day in response to an urgent request from the government. Emotional support and socialization were provided by groups of volunteers to isolated elderly people. Volunteers also delivered masks, sanitation products, and food. Importantly, they also provided information on transmission prevention. They helped people feel less isolated and

---

* Benjamin Lough, "Recognizing the Value of Volunteering in Resilient Communities," *IAVE Volunteering Together Magazine*, no. 7 (May 2020): https://www.iave.org/volunteering-together-magazine/issue-7/.

alone and developed an antivirus project to encourage and facilitate nongovernmental organizations (NGOs) and volunteer groups to organize volunteer services focused on caring for the most vulnerable.

AVS emphasized collaborating to avoid duplication with nongovernmental organizations (NGOs) and public authorities to make sure those most in need were given priority. They also worked in partnership with a charitable trust and other donors to release funds to support volunteer services and enable volunteers to access the appropriate protective materials to maximize their safety.

A Wave of Informal Volunteers in Rome (CSV Lazio)

In Rome, the pandemic created three key volunteering challenges: the immediate loss of a committed cohort of older volunteers who were considered most at risk, the risk to vulnerable elderly people through lack of access to food, medicine, essential services, and the economic challenge, and hardship for people newly without work. These situations were already precarious before the pandemic but became even more difficult.

The key strategies that worked included supporting an upsurge in informal and self-organized volunteering and engaging young people to help. Volunteers reacted immediately by creating a network to organize food deliveries and providing a safety net that prevented the economic crisis from causing a complete societal breakdown.

This process also required the wave of informal volunteers that came forward to help and self-organize. These volunteers were often young and "digitally native" (meaning they grew up with digital technology and were already intimately familiar with it), and they became ideal informal responders. This informal volunteering was most successful when delivered within local communities and coordinated by the local government to ensure collaboration between the third sector and informal volunteers. CSV Lazio supported this engagement of informal and formal volunteering, understanding that the community's capacity for resilience requires a joint effort of local partners.

The Learning: More Knowledge-Sharing Needed

COVID-19 became a pandemic that caused a global crisis, thus requiring a global response. Volunteers were often frontline responders, either through an organization or informally through neighborliness and individual community action.

The pandemic has caused change and challenge. Leadership for volunteering organizations have had to adapt to new realities such as virtual volunteering and embrace this as a part of their future. The mobilization of volunteers remains a key priority, especially as we need volunteers now more than ever to meet current and future societal challenges.

The engagement of individuals through volunteering is vital to building resilient communities that will help all of us prepare for the next crisis. This includes reenergizing existing volunteers, recruiting younger generations, and developing volunteer leadership. We need to adapt to create space for both formal and informal volunteering—to create a volunteer movement in solidarity with itself. It also means being mindful of diversity and inclusivity as the hallmarks of our volunteer strategies.

Leadership for volunteering organizations understand that the effective management of volunteers maximizes impact and that during the pandemic, a wealth of good practice has been developed. Networking and the global sharing of information, experience, and expertise are important to maximize use of available resources and enhance effectiveness. IAVE's Global Network for Volunteering Leadership (GNVL)* is an example of this in practice. IAVE believes it is imperative that others also recognize that information and knowledge-sharing enable volunteering to flourish worldwide.

COVID-19 has been a disruptive force that challenged volunteering leadership and the entire global volunteering family. It continues to create a sense of uncertainty and unpredictability about what the future will hold. Within this maelstrom, there is one important hopeful reflection: "Volunteering is a fundamental building block of civil society. It brings to life the noblest aspirations of humankind—the pursuit of peace, freedom, opportunity, safety and justice for all people."†

---

*   International Association for Volunteer Effort, "Global Network of Volunteering Leadership," IAVE, accessed 2021, https://www.iave.org/gnvl/.

†   Universal Declaration on Volunteering, Adopted by the international board of directors of IAVE at its sixteenth World Volunteer Conference, Amsterdam, the Netherlands, January 2001, the International Year of Volunteers, https://www.iave.org/advocacy/the-universal-declaration-on-volunteering/.

Connecting Volunteers to Organizations: Learnings from the COVID-19 Pandemic

Laura Plato

Laura Plato is a certified professional coach and entrepreneur with over twenty years of experience leading transformational change for nonprofit and for-profit organizations. A nationally published author, speaker, and advisor in the field of social impact, she has appeared on NBC, NPR, and CNN, as well as in dozens of other global forums. In her role as Chief Solutions Officer for VolunteerMatch, she spearheaded strategic partnerships with organizations including Apple, Creative Artists Agency, and California Volunteers. Other recent work includes leveraging investments and cross-sector data to increase capacity for Black, Indigenous, and People of Color (BIPOC)-led nonprofits and to understand COVID-19's impact on volunteering.

* * *

"The impatient idealist says: 'Give me a place to stand and I
shall move the earth.' But such a place does not exist. We all
have to stand on the earth itself and go with her at her pace."

—Chinua Achebe, *No Longer at Ease*

It's March 2020, and our VolunteerMatch team stands at the
crossroads of mission and stark reality.

Ninety-three percent of all volunteering has just been
reported "canceled."[*]

This datapoint, culled from our first round of pandemic
volunteering-related research, is, to say the least, unexpected.
Like so much of the news during these early days, it's both
initially shocking and subsequently heartbreaking. We cannot
help but project forward to imagine the long-term implications
of a nation suddenly devoid of volunteering.

In the over two-decades-long history of VolunteerMatch—a
nonprofit organization whose sole mission is to connect
would-be volunteers with causes that will benefit from their
time and talents—we have never faced a volunteering decline
anywhere near as dramatic as this. In the United States, where
most of our day-to-day operational efforts are focused, we are
accustomed to a relative flood of passionate volunteers; on
average, over a million seek out VolunteerMatch opportunities every month. They talk about the organization on social
media and share volunteer opportunities with friends. I can't
count the number of times a random stranger has told me on

---

[*]   VolunteerMatch, *Volunteering During COVID-19* (VolunteerMatch: https://
info.volunteermatch.org/volunteering-during-covid-ebook).

an airplane that VolunteerMatch is the first place they learned about where they can donate their time to their local community. In a country where about a quarter of the population* volunteers every year and where 80 percent of nonprofits rely on those volunteers† to achieve their missions, Volunteer-Match has carved out a unique niche connecting impassioned volunteers with meaningful causes.

With the early data in, a stark new reality emerges: to fulfill its mission, our organization must completely pivot its business plan.

An End to "Business as Usual" Demands a Commitment to "Voice of Customer"

In early 2020, relying heavily on this research, VolunteerMatch made the decision to shift the focus of the entire organization to three key areas:

1. Build a new online hub that encourages people to connect and share COVID-specific volunteering best practices, research, and other human connection-oriented resources.

---

* Bureau of Labor Statistics, "Volunteering in the United States—2015," U.S. Department of Labor, published February 25, 2016, https://www.bls.gov/news.release/pdf/volun.pdf.

† The Urban Institute, "Volunteer Management Capacity in America's Charities and Congregations: A Briefing Report," The Urban Institute, published 2004, http://webarchive.urban.org/UploadedPDF/410963_VolunteerManagment.pdf.

2. Enhance technology capabilities to effectively foster COVID-specific and virtual volunteering engagements across local, regional, national, and global lines.

3. Develop an advocacy platform to offer a trustworthy space for conversations about social justice to occur to ensure the inevitable inequities faced by our BIPOC communities during COVID and opportunities to serve in solidarity are surfaced for would-be volunteers.

Embracing its role as a connector and concentrating on building highly accessible, relevant advocacy and technology platforms during a time of constantly changing norms necessitated that VolunteerMatch become more committed to listening to customers and partners than ever before.

The team took up the challenge to extend the initial volume of research performed in March into a quarterly series conducted in May, July, and October 2020, to reach thousands of nonprofits, volunteers, and businesses and understand, from their point of view, what their experience was really like day-to-day during COVID-19. Throughout 2020, the team published these results to a global audience to raise awareness of how the social sector was performing throughout the crisis and ensure needed funding and support would continue to flow.

In total, this research obtained nearly fifty-six hundred submissions from nonprofits, businesses, government organizations, consultants, and volunteers who answered the same series of questions around volunteerism. In full transparency, despite these significant returns, there remains much to do and much to learn from these customers.

Here are four urgent themes that emerged from the research, along with some thoughts on what remains to be explored more deeply:

One: Recruitment Practices Shifted Dramatically

During COVID-19, the concept of "hybrid volunteering models," in which in-person volunteering experiences can flow into virtual experiences and back again seamlessly, emerged to encourage continuous volunteer engagement—but, despite this development, a mismatch persisted between organizational and volunteer needs.

In March 2020, despite deep uncertainty about the pandemic, over 50 percent of volunteers said they still wanted to help in-person, while 44 percent expressed an interest in helping virtually. During that same month, 32 percent of nonprofit respondents stated that they had begun to create virtual volunteering opportunities in response to perceived demand. This number grew to 51 percent by October.

VolunteerMatch witnessed persistent pressure throughout the pandemic on nonprofits, including itself, to create additional virtual volunteering opportunities. Equally, as a technology provider, VolunteerMatch welcomed the interest in the systems and tools that promised to improve access to those opportunities. And, in its role as advocate and storyteller, the organization received consistent outreach to highlight the successes, particularly from well-intentioned corporations, media outlets, and philanthropic funders.

Despite all this intense focus across every aspect of the

landscape on virtual volunteering, in the final study in October* the team learned that only 29 percent of volunteers reported having actually participated in virtual opportunities since the beginning of the COVID-19 crisis.

The question remains worthy of study: *how will recruiting practices evolve?* Will there continue to be pressure to operate in a hybrid mode, allowing for continuity across in-person and virtual volunteering experiences, or will volunteers and circumstances demand a stronger preference for one or the other? Certainly, some forms of transactional volunteering seem ripe for a full-time move to online or virtual. One avenue for exploration is in transferable lessons learned from e-commerce,† which could offer interesting insights into the benefits of an ongoing commitment to understanding and designing for the entire volunteer lifecycle.

Two: Interest Does Not Necessarily Equal Activation

If you could travel back to December 2019, prepandemic, you'd be able to join over nine million people who visited volunteermatch.org to discover volunteer opportunities that year. Just one year later, VolunteerMatch network data revealed that one point two million fewer people invested in opportunity searches during the pandemic.

---

*   VolunteerMatch, "2020 in Review: The Impact of COVID-19 on the Social Sector," VolunteerMatch, accessed 2021, https://info.volunteermatch.org/2020-in-review-the-impact-of-covid-19-on-volunteering-the-social-sector.

†   Kathy Gramlin et al., "How E-Commerce Fits into Retail's Postpandemic Future," Harvard Business Review, published May 11, 2021, https://hbr.org/2021/05/how-e-commerce-fits-into-retails-post-pandemic-future.

These numbers began to slowly recover in the latter part of 2020 and throughout 2021. Simultaneously, however, as volunteerism struggled, the average number of nonprofits posting volunteer opportunities grew and the number of "volunteers needed" ranged between six to eight million consistently across 2020 and 2021. This decline in the searching and matching of over one million volunteers massively impacts already underserved nonprofits who simply may not receive the volunteer connections they need in time. This delta highlights the tenuousness of the fabric of volunteering exacerbated by the disruption of the pandemic, and, again, an interesting potential area for future behavioral study.

Three: Fear and Regulations Were Major Barriers

"Tenuousness" relates to a third theme: *Fear and regulations were major barriers to volunteering and deepened isolation and relational loss for both volunteers and constituents.*

VolunteerMatch deploys digital infrastructure (systems, tools, and sites) to serve every nonprofit cause—a role that puts it in a unique position to witness some of the less rosy impacts on volunteers and the constituents who benefit from volunteer service.

Immediate and deep losses showed up across several cause areas, including mentoring, library volunteering, and hospice—areas where in-person volunteering is the norm. Volunteering also dropped off among many volunteer populations, including volunteers aged fifty-five and older, workplace volunteers subject to shifting corporate volunteering policies, and individual volunteers seeking to support cause areas that were forced to cease in-person operations, such as art museums, churches, and schools. In these areas, volunteering dropped off, impacting network connections.

One unique barrier to volunteering that study respondents shared consistently throughout the pandemic was "exposing other people to illness." This fear persisted—and actually grew worse—throughout the year.* While only 46 percent of respondents shared this concern in March, by October, the number had grown steadily to 62 percent. Many volunteers, fearful of becoming ill themselves, refrained from searching for new, nonprofit-sponsored volunteer experiences, choosing instead to offer their support to smaller, neighbor-to-neighbor, grassroots-led, and mutual aid efforts characterized as safely distanced and often rooted in the local community.†

Volunteering ethicists have long cautioned, appropriately, that a guiding principle for volunteers should be "do no harm."‡ During the pandemic, fear of exposing others or being exposed to illness underlined this precept. Yet, more initially subtle but ultimately long-ranging effects are also being felt today, because of further isolation and relational losses for constituents. Research in the sector is just beginning to reveal the long-term effects of how 2020 has impacted volunteers and those they help. Student populations who lost both in-person schooling and volunteer-led after-school

---

* VolunteerMatch, "2020 in Review," 13.

† Christine Fernando, "Mutual Aid Networks Find Roots in Communities of Color," AP News, published January 21, 2021, https://apnews.com/article/immigration-coronavirus-pandemic-7b1d14f25ab717c2a29ceafd40364b6e.

‡ Jean Rhodes et al., "First Do No Harm," *Professional Psychology: Research and Practice* 40, no 5 (2009): 452–458, http://rhodeslab.org/files/EthicsAPA.pdf.

programs, along with tutoring and mentoring relationships[*] may very well experience lasting impacts. Equally, volunteers ages fifty-five and older, for whom volunteer service is an important part of day-to-day life,[†] warrant attention in terms of possible lasting impacts on their mental and physical well-being.

Four: Equitable Access Has a Long Way to Go

Finally: *The disruption of the pandemic exacerbated existing cracks in the system, revealing that equitable access for volunteers and nonprofit staffers still has a long way to go.*

2020 was not only a year of adapting to a pandemic. It was a year of much-overdue racial reckoning. While initially, many causes and technologists embraced a laser focus on virtual and pandemic-oriented activities, any of these interventions not grounded in equity and justice occurs as both tone-deaf and destined to produce suboptimal outcomes.

Demand for COVID-related volunteer opportunities never ranged as high as demand for human rights, racial-, and social justice–oriented opportunities in the VolunteerMatch network. Traditional virtual volunteering as a tool to offer support on a global scale quickly resolved into a demand for local-as-virtual opportunities that would allow a volunteer to provide support within their own zip code, or even, on their own street,

---

[*] Per Engzell et al., "Learning Loss Due to School Closures during the COVID-19 Pandemic," *PNAS* 118, no. 17 (April 27, 2021): https://doi.org/10.1073/pnas.2022376118.

[†] Marcia Fearn et al., "Befriending Older Adults in Nursing Homes: Volunteer Perceptions of Switching to Remote Befriending in the COVID-19 Era," *Clinical Gerontologist* 44, no. 4 (2021): 430–438, doi: 10.1080/07317115.2020.1868646.

representing a deepening awareness and commitment to the idea that inequity begins at home.

In some cases, organizing technologies were simply unavailable, unable to reorient, or unappealing. In others, a deep internal need to "do something" leapfrogged research and discovery and moved directly into creating and doing. As a result, we saw the emergence of grassroots mutual aid movements, organized around principles and systems characterized by easy-to-use, often low-fi, technologies and distributed leadership.* While a few of these mutual aid movements went on to formalize their status and organize as 501c3 nonprofits, many did not and will not, yet they continue to exist and provide valuable services in parallel to the traditional nonprofit structure.

Human Connection, Interrupted

While some people cite the issues inherent in these loosely held, lightly policed groups—including long-term viability, opportunity for impact measurement, and security—mutual aid groups that emerged during the pandemic continue to successfully thrive and adapt.† While much work remains, technology providers including VolunteerMatch continue to explore ways to support the spirit and potential of these movements with noncommercial technology solutions that

---

*   Jia Tolentino, "What Mutual Aid Can Do During a Pandemic," The New Yorker, May 18, 2020, https://www.newyorker.com/magazine/2020/05/18/what-mutual-aid-can-do-during-a-pandemic.

†   Arden Sklar, "A Year and a Half into the Pandemic, NYC's Mutual Aid Movement at a Turning Point," City Limits, published September 24, 2021, https://citylimits.org/2021/09/24/a-year-and-a-half-into-pandemic-nycs-mutual-aid-movement-at-a-turning-point/.

could help ease some of the challenges while enhancing the likelihood of long-term impact and success.

Fundamentally, the story of how the pandemic affected the ways volunteers connected to causes is a story of fundamental human connection, interrupted. Technology can play a vital role in facilitating certain connections, but, as we saw with the successes of hyper-local, grassroots, and mutual aid movements during the pandemic, in places like the VolunteerMatch Slack Community* and in the delta between what research respondents said they wanted and what they actually did, virtual will not, and should not, be treated as a panacea for all that ills us when in-person connection becomes difficult or impossible.

If there is a legacy of the pandemic on volunteer connections it is this: our *presence*—mindful, conscious, human presence— is required to promote healthy, thriving communities. Virtual, digital, and asynchronous engagements can play complementary supporting roles during times of disruption. But, in our quest for continuity, improvement, and impact, where we inspire activation and engagement through faster, better, and smarter technology, we must never lose sight of this essential truth. It is through mindful, human presence that we bear witness to one another in all our messy, joyous, and inspired humanity, and in the process grow to understand and connect to one another, ourselves, and our world more deeply.

---

*   VolunteerMatch Slack Collaborative, https://volunteermatc-rt64629. slack.com/join/shared_invite/zt-dvyi315x-aW3nUiotKwNlrS46Fc7RNA#/ shared-invite/email.

Racial Equity in Volunteerism

Wendy Vang-Roberts

Wendy Vang-Roberts (she/her) is a first-generation Hmong American from Minnesota who is dedicated to taking action to dismantle racism and inequities through training, storytelling, and creating spaces for meaningful dialogue. She is the Training Director at the Minnesota Alliance for Volunteer Advancement (MAVA) where she manages professional development for volunteer engagement leaders. Wendy has worked in a variety of adult student, volunteer, and national service outreach and volunteer engagement leader support and training roles. Wendy holds a master of public and nonprofit administration from Metropolitan State University and serves on the Antiracism Study Dialogue Circles (ASDIC) Metamorphosis Board and Marketing Committee and Asian American Organizing Project (AAOP) Board.

* * *

When I first started my journey as a volunteer engagement professional, I noticed something slightly off-putting—something that made me feel like an outlier: most of the volunteers I engaged didn't look like me. The volunteers didn't bear resemblance to those in the community we served, either.

I am a first-generation Hmong American from Minneapolis. I joined the Minnesota Alliance for Volunteer Advancement (MAVA) as the Training Manager in the fall of 2020 where much of my work has included racial equity. But prior to that, I managed statewide volunteer and adult student outreach at a nonprofit organization focused on education, which required that we engage volunteers to tutor or instruct adult students. Many of these students were Black, Indigenous, people of color (BIPOC), and immigrants or refugees.

It likely won't come as a surprise for many to hear that our volunteer corps was predominantly white; only 11 percent of volunteers were BIPOC. This demographic makeup is not unique to the education field. While the creation of this homogenous environment wasn't intentional—we didn't purposefully and intentionally seek white-only volunteers—there are strong biases at play that have ultimately influenced the homogenous nature of the organization's structure. This stems back to the white supremacy culture that has permeated our society since our nation's founding.

Unfortunately, this is an underlying theme within the nonprofit sector at large that has profound effects on who volunteers and how they do it. And while this is something we may have all felt and seen, it wasn't really a focus for the nonprofit sector broadly, nor the volunteer engagement field that supported the sector prior to 2020. There wasn't a real thirst to understand what was causing this.

Prior to 2020, there were strong indications that nearly half of nonprofit organizations in the United States didn't even have a formal diversity statement, according to a 2019 Nonprofit Diversity Practices Report published by Nonprofit HR.* Even worse, this same report revealed that nearly 70 percent of nonprofits didn't have an actively applied diversity strategy. We should acknowledge that racial equity is everyone's responsibility, but with only 22 percent of organizations indicating they have a staff person whose role is solely focused on diversity efforts, it's clear that racial equity was on the back burner.†

Similar trends can be seen at the practitioner's level, as some of the toughest challenges expressed by volunteer engagement professionals in the Volunteer Pro 2020 Volunteer Management Report included recruiting the "right volunteers for specific roles and needs," getting buy-in "from coworkers and leadership," time management against competing priorities within their respective organizations, designing volunteer roles to meet organizational needs and of course, the lost art of retention and maintaining commitments from longtime volunteers.‡ Of those listed, recruitment and buy-in have surfaced

---

*   Nonprofit HR, "2019 Nonprofit Diversity Practices Report," Nonprofit HR, accessed 2021, nonprofithr.com/2019diversityreport.
†   Nonprofit HR, "2019 Nonprofit Diversity Practices Report."
‡   Tobi Johnson et al., "Volunteer Management Progress Report, January 16, 2020," Volunteer Pro, published 2020, https://s3.amazonaws.com/kaja-bi-storefronts-production/sites/60619/themes/1474670/downloads/AjAs-WxeJScqktfA7nkR1_2020_VMPR_Report_FINAL_v3.pdf.

as the top two needs over the span of three consecutive years.[*]

Additionally, there were many themes within the context of nonprofit volunteer engagement that were top of mind for organizations that engaged volunteers. The nonprofit sector as a whole has been incredibly reliant on older volunteers, which had implications on the use of technology. Long-term volunteering had been eroding even prior to the pandemic. Lastly—and important to note—nonprofit organizations are effusive about monetary benefits volunteers bring to their organizations.[†] For example, volunteers who brought benefit to the organization's bottom line are more highly prized than those who don't.[‡]

The Day the World Changed Forever

As you can see, prior to 2020, racial equity was less of a focus for the nonprofit sector, and almost unacknowledged as it relates to volunteerism and those who work as professionals in that field. Racial equity wasn't even in the conversation or a recognized theme within volunteerism.

This changed dramatically in the summer of 2020.

Society's support for (and interest in) racial justice changed

---

[*]   Tobi Johnson et al., "Volunteer Management Progress Report, January 16, 2020."

[†]   Mark A. Hager and Jeffrey L. Brudney, "Volunteer Management Capacity in America's Charities: Benchmarking a Prepandemic Field and Assessing Future Direction," April 2021, https://www.volunteeralive.org/docs/Hager_Brudney_VMC2_2021_brief.pdf.

[‡]   Mark A. Hager and Jeffrey L. Brudney, "Volunteer Management Capacity in America's Charities: Benchmarking a Prepandemic Field and Assessing Future Direction."

overnight after the murder of George Floyd, which was captured on video for the world to see. Amid a global pandemic, the world watched a white Minneapolis police officer kneel on Floyd's neck for nine minutes and twenty-nine seconds[*] as he pleaded for his life, sparking massive protests and global racial reckoning.

Floyd's murder happened in my community—Minneapolis. I both witnessed and participated in one of the largest mobilizations of people around a single cause—racial justice—the nation has ever seen. This included protests, cleaning up after the riots and vandalism, community gatherings, and even more grassroots activities and localized acts of service like donating food and supplies for those in need. Just like that, racial justice moved to a national spotlight in the United States. I wondered—and still wonder—just how long this energy will last. Regardless, one thing is certain: The conversation about racial equity has never been as loud and pronounced as it is now in the field of volunteer engagement.

In the weeks following Floyd's murder, many institutions—from small nonprofits to large corporations—published statements affirming their commitment to racial justice. It became popular to offer training sessions, promote book clubs focused on race and racism, and virtual coffee breaks discussing racial justice. Everyone seemed to be waking up to the historical and ongoing systemic racism that has been deeply ingrained into our society.

---

[*]   Eric Levenson, "Former Officer Knelt on George Floyd for Nine Minutes and Twenty-Nine Seconds—Not the Infamous 8:46," Central News Network, Published March 30, 2021, https://www.cnn.com/2021/03/29/us/george-floyd-timing-929-846/index.html.

Nonprofit leaders across the globe—including many volunteer engagement professionals—turned to MAVA because we had been researching and advocating for racial equity in volunteerism long before Floyd's death. Since mid-2020, MAVA has received an unprecedented interest in training and consulting services for nonprofit organizations that want to dismantle structural racism in volunteerism while also building cultural awareness among their employees and volunteers.

In prepandemic years, MAVA typically offered six to eleven racial equity workshops averaging 275 total attendees per year. With the increased interest in racial equity coupled with virtual capabilities, we have delivered more than thirty-six Diversity Equity and Inclusion (DEI) and racial equity workshops, engaging over two thousand participants in 2021 alone. This rapid rise in interest and attendance tells us that many organizations are beginning to take steps toward racial justice.

To reinforce this point, through the research conducted by MAVA, we found that many nonprofit and government organizations struggle to engage volunteers who reflect the communities they serve. Through a series of eight listening sessions that took place between November 2020 and March 2021,* BIPOC volunteers shared that the very systems created to engage volunteers present barriers that in many instances prevent would-be volunteers from serving.

---

* Karmit Bulman, "Cocreating Racial Equity in Volunteer Engagement—Learning from Listening Sessions with Black, Indigenous, and People of Color," Minnesota Alliance for Volunteer Advancement, August 20, 2021, https://mava.clubexpress.com/content.aspx?page_id=2507&club_id=286912&item_id=3647.

These barriers are not unique to any one organization. In fact, these barriers were erected and put in place as "best practices," many of which are familiar to us—such as applications, orientations, training, interviews, background checks, and screening procedures. Many of these practices that were originally designed to ensure proper placement and mitigate risk are not inclusive. In some ways, these practices actually reinforce systems of power and privilege, thereby inadvertently excluding historically marginalized communities.

Since Floyd's murder and the resulting heightened awareness of racial equity, many organizations have sought to take steps to operationalize racial equity in volunteerism. But I often remind folks that this work isn't about simply checking a box; it requires intentionality. It requires endurance, time, commitment, and support from the highest level.

Many organizations that started this journey back in 2020 are still working and will be for years to come—as they should be. Of course, organizations implement many practices, but some of the most fruitful we've seen adopted, practiced, and refined include the foundational step of collecting volunteer demographics, the adoption and use of inclusive language, and investment in Diversity, Equity, and Inclusion (DEI) training for volunteers and employees.

Understanding Who Volunteers Is Key

This isn't a commonly adopted tactic, but it's important. Prior to working at MAVA, in my capacity as a volunteer engagement practitioner, one of the first steps I took in working toward racial equity was to improve our collection and evaluation of volunteer demographic data. To advance racial equity, we needed to find out whose voices are missing and why; the data helped us find answers.

Through our work, we engaged more than thirty-five hundred volunteers annually, and while I didn't know every volunteer personally, of the many volunteers I did know, very few were BIPOC. By collecting demographic data, we accomplished three things: we identified how few BIPOC volunteers we had, we created a form of accountability to help secure buy-in from leaders, and we made it harder to overlook those in the minority. This is naturally where most organizations should start.

Communicate in Ways That Are Universally Understood

One organization MAVA has worked with and learned from is Tubman, an organization that provides safe shelter and support to people of all ages, genders, and cultural backgrounds who are struggling with relationship violence, substance abuse, mental health, and other forms of trauma. Racial equity has been at the forefront for Tubman staff for years—long before the murder of Floyd. They request demographics from volunteers during their training rather than during their application process. This ensures that volunteers know their information will not be used to screen them out. It also allows for more accurate tracking of who is actually volunteering, as applications do not necessarily reflect retention. With this data, Tubman has found that they have been successful in attracting and retaining BIPOC volunteers. Measurement is important, and the data collected helps track progress and assess whether the desired results are being achieved.

Like many other fields, the volunteerism field is filled with language that may alienate people. Take, for example, the word "volunteer." This word is not universally understood; it doesn't even exist in some languages and is often used to describe formal volunteering. That said, many people, such as BIPOC, give their time in other ways not commonly understood as volunteering (i.e., grassroots advocacy, neighbor-to-neighbor, peer-to-peer, and directly to members of the community). With the gift of their time, they drive neighbors or friends to appointments, cook meals for friends, provide childcare while parents are at work. Additionally, words like "help," "assist" and "work with" more closely reflect how BIPOC communities share their time.*

In another experience from Literacy Minnesota—an organization with whom MAVA worked closely—we also noticed that acts of service that benefit the community were more valued than language that indicated a benefit to the organization. Using the tips on language MAVA developed as a starting point, my former team and I revised the organization's volunteer recruitment message. We changed language like "meet people from around the world" to "meet people from your community" to remove stereotypes or assumptions about who can volunteer. We also highlighted in our messages that no prior experience is needed,

---

*   Karmit Bulman, "Cocreating Racial Equity in Volunteer Engagement—Learning from Listening Sessions with Black, Indigenous, and People of Color," Minnesota Alliance for Volunteer Advancement, August 20, 2021, https://mava.clubexpress.com/content.aspx?page_id=2507&club_id=286912&item_id=3647.

and all training is provided. Prospective volunteers regularly shared that they didn't realize they could volunteer with us without a college degree or some form of teaching experience. Language is powerful and easy to misinterpret; even the slightest changes to a word choice can transform its entire message.

DEI Training and Professional Development for Volunteers

An additional trend includes organizations providing racial equity and other DEI training for its employees. However, only in some instances have volunteers been invited to participate in this important training, which is alarming. Because many volunteers engage directly with communities, it is crucial that they are included in the organization's DEI education and training efforts to build awareness of bias and how biases can show up in interactions with others.

Consider this example: With MAVA's support and guidance, Girls on the Run Minnesota (GOTR), a nonprofit organization that inspires girls through physical activity, held listening sessions with their current BIPOC volunteers. Their feedback revealed that the volunteer corps, which is predominantly white, would benefit greatly from DEI training.

GOTR incorporated training on how to avoid microaggressions into their regular required volunteer trainings and have since started having braver conversations using real-life scenarios. Their BIPOC volunteers have shared that they appreciate GOTR's transparency and feel comfortable going to their supervisor with issues. White volunteers have also shared that they have since learned that some of their behaviors were harmful to BIPOC. At GOTR, training is not simply seen as a "check a box" activity, but as a way to develop shared language and steppingstones to dismantle racial inequities—a good lesson for all organizations considering DEI training for their volunteers.

I'd be lying if I said we—those of us in the nonprofit sector—have it all figured out. The truth is, while racial equity has been an issue for hundreds of years, this journey by the nonprofit sector leadership and the field of volunteer engagement is very much in its infancy compared to other professions and sectors.

Who Else, What More, and What Other?

The truth of the matter is that not much has changed since Floyd's death. For example, according to the 2021 Nonprofit Diversity Practices report, only 21 percent of respondents reported having a dedicated staff member whose role is responsible for its DEI efforts.[*] I must point out this number is actually one percent lower than reported in 2019. A second reminder from this same report indicates that only about half of the nonprofits surveyed have staff who reflect the communities they serve. Lastly, as it relates to the field of volunteer engagement, I'm sharply reminded that beyond the mechanisms created to engage volunteers in service, the professional makeup of those within volunteer engagement—as leaders engaging volunteers in their respective organizations—is still largely homogeneous. It's estimated that more than 84 percent

---

[*] Emily Holthaus et al., "2021 Nonprofit Diversity practices Report," Nonprofit HR, 2021, https://www.nonprofithr.com/wp-content/uploads/2021/04/2021-Diversity-Report-Project-Final-Published-1.pdf.

of volunteer engagement leaders identify as white, Caucasian, or of European descent.* So, there's much, much more work to be done even within our own ranks.

The good news is that we have learned many lessons since 2020. It will take a real and sustained effort by leadership to prioritize the ongoing issue of equity. And while words are great, *action is better*. There's a real opportunity for CEOs, Executive Directors, and other leaders within the nonprofit sector to make a real stand, and to elevate this conversation to a much higher level of priority.

I've learned a lot through the years as a practitioner working toward racial equity in volunteerism, but the one resounding lesson applicable to everyone is this: Begin this journey where you have direct control and can invite people—your peers, direct reports, and leadership, both at your organization and from partner organizations—to join in the work.

I've been told many times to "never let a crisis go to waste." We are in a racial crisis in the United States. We must not let this crisis go to waste. Achieving racial equity is lifelong work; it requires thoughtful consideration, intention-setting, planning, and execution. We're only beginning to scratch the surface.

Our work does not end here.

---

* Tobi Johnson et al., "Volunteer Management Progress Report, January 16, 2020.," 15.

Co-Generational Service: A Disruption to Increase Impact

Phyllis N. Segal

Phyllis N. Segal is a Senior Fellow at Encore.org, a national nonprofit dedicated to bridging generational divides. She has led initiatives and written extensively on both the encore stage of life and national civilian service. Appointed by President Barack Obama and confirmed by the U.S. Senate, Phyllis served as a board member of the Corporation for National and Community Service.*

Americans witnessed in 2020 the largest increase in poverty in six decades. School shutdowns have caused learning losses that could hobble an entire generation. Social isolation has

---

*   This article is adapted from P. Segal, "Intergenerational National Service By, With and For All Ages," *eJournal of Public Affairs Missouri State University*, 10, no. 2 (July 2021), http://www.ejournalofpublicaffairs.org/intergenerational-national-service-by-with-and-for-all-ages/.

exacerbated loneliness, most seriously affecting the mental health of younger and older adults. While deep divisions existed well before the pandemic, the risk they pose to American democracy brings new urgency to bridging them.

One of the divides thwarting social cohesion is between generations; it is driven by social isolation, instability, and fear. In public and private discourse at the beginning of the pandemic, young people were blamed for spreading the virus, while the higher risk of death for older adults was seen as driving shutdowns. This sticky narrative pitted generations against each other. Compounded by the divergent economic effects of COVID-19 on older and younger people, it has fueled an outbreak of ageism,* adversely affecting old and young alike.

Connecting older and younger people to work together to meet community needs can help heal fractures and address social problems. Historian Anne Applebaum, writing in *The Atlantic*, proposed that the best way to bridge divides is by bringing people together to do something constructive, focusing on their common purpose.† Age-integrating our volunteer and civilian national service workforces is an effective way to do this. It requires recruiting participants of different ages and bringing them together for meaningful interaction. The power of co-generational service is seen where this is happening.

---

* Liat Ayalon et al, "Aging in Times of the COVID-19 Pandemic: Avoiding Ageism and Fostering Intergenerational Solidarity." *The Journals of Gerontology: Series B* 76, no. 2 (February 2021): e49–e52, https://doi.org/10.1093/geronb/gbaa051.

† Anne Applebaum, "Coexistence is the Only Option." The Atlantic, published January 20, 2021, https://www.theatlantic.com/ideas/archive/2021/01/seditionists-need-path-back-society/617746/.

Melanie Rudolph served on an AmeriCorps team with SBP, a national disaster recovery organization. In addition to Melanie, who is in her sixties, the team included others in their twenties. The team worked together to rebuild homes destroyed by hurricanes. Melanie's AmeriCorps team brought people of different ages together, building bonds through intergenerational volunteering. Strangers before this experience, she discovered "I would do anything for them, just like they would do anything for me. We're like a well-oiled machine. You know, everybody has their gifts and skills, and we recognize that and support each other."*

This approach to volunteering and civilian national service disrupts age segregation in our civic life, helps build bridges across widening divides, and increases our ability to solve problems from climate change to loneliness.

A New Approach

In addition to team-based programs like SBP, co-generational service is also possible in programs like the Stockton Service Corps (SSC), where participants work individually but come together in cohorts to learn from and about each other. But in both programs, and many others, the intergenerational mix and meaningful interaction is typically not by design. SBP, for example, did not set out to recruit members from different age groups—only 5 percent of those working on its disaster relief teams are fifty or older.

---

* Gen2Gen, 2021, "I love working on a multigenerational team," Facebook, February 1, 2021, https://www.facebook.com/iamGen2Gen/posts/2784850155069001.

If co-generational service can occur organically in programs like SBP and SSC, imagine the potential if programs followed an intentional strategy to recruit and engage people from various stages of life to work together toward a common goal. It's time to do more than imagine. Intentional intergenerational service can seize opportunities created by changing demographics and counter problems exacerbated by the pandemic. When adopted, these practices will benefit participants, strengthen communities, and perhaps even unite us as a nation.

It is not a surprise that age segregation is common in programs that engage volunteers and national service members, just as it pervades every major aspect of American life. Over the past century, our country changed from being one of the most age-integrated societies in the world to one of the most age-segregated.

As Marc Freedman and Trent Stamp explained in the Stanford Social Innovation Review, age-segregation "was driven by well-intentioned public policies and social innovations aimed at achieving greater efficiency and solving major problems."* They point to how universal education and child labor laws led to schools putting same-age students together in classrooms, Social Security and mandatory retirement helped dislodge older employees from the workforce amid high Depression-era unemployment rates, and retirement communities and senior centers kept older adults involved mostly with their peers.

---

* Marc Freedman and Trent Stamp, "Overcoming Age Segregation," Stanford Social Innovation Review (March 15, 2021): https://ssir.org/articles/entry/overcoming_age_segregation#.

Service programs have largely echoed the resulting age-seg-regation norm. The alphabet soup of service programs enacted by Congress over the past century includes many that limited participation to defined age groups. For example, in 1933, the Civilian Conservation Corps (CCC) limited participation to eighteen to twenty-five-year-olds. Sixty years later, the National Civilian Community Corps (NCCC), limited eligibility to young adults between the ages of eighteen and twenty-four.

At the other end of the age spectrum are three service programs created in the mid-1960s that limited participation to older adults. The Foster Grandparent Program (FGP), Senior Companions, and the Retired and Senior Volunteer Program (RSVP) were part of President Lyndon Johnson's Great Society antipoverty initiatives to tap the skills, talents, and experience of older Americans.

There also are civilian national service programs, like the Peace Corps, Volunteers in Service to America (VISTA) and AmeriCorps State and National, that were never limited by law to defined age groups. And yet, in practice, even these programs have been largely age-segregated. In 2018, only 5 percent of AmeriCorps members were fifty-five or older. The same year, the median age of Peace Corps volunteers in 2018 was twenty-five; only 3 percent were fifty-six or older.

Structures have reinforced separation. In the federal agency that oversees all the domestic civilian national service programs, those that engage different age groups have oper-ated in distinct silos. For example, RSVP and other Senior Corps programs, on the one hand, and AmeriCorps direct service programs on the other, often operate in the same communities without any interaction among programs or service members. As a recent welcome harbinger of change, these programs in 2020 were rebranded under the singular "AmeriCorps" umbrella and there have been modest steps taken to promote collaboration between members in RSVP, AmeriCorps State and NCCC programs.

In addition to disrupting the pattern of age-segregated service, these steps begin to carry out what Congress originally intended in laws passed over the past two decades. For example, the National and Community Service Trust Act of 1993 encouraged newly created AmeriCorps programs to include intergenerational service. Age-integrated team service was first on the list of models eligible for funding.

Learning from One Another

Co-generational service—where older and younger people work alongside each other to meet community needs—is a type of intergenerational service. This approach (1) changes attitudes about those who are older and younger, (2) strengthens the effectiveness of service programs, and (3) maximizes the numbers of people who serve.

Older and younger people describe how serving together changed their thinking and attitudes about each other. For twenty-four-year-old AmeriCorps SBP member Emerson Jordan-Wood, serving on a team with an AmeriCorps member in her seventies was "an opportunity to break down some of my pre-existing stereotypes about older people." As he explained, "I felt nervous about telling Miss Laurie that I use they/them as pronouns [...] But there was this one day on-site, when I was getting comfortable and talking with some people about some of the changes I was seeing after being on testosterone. She overheard me and was like, 'Okay, there it is! I knew you'd eventually be comfortable enough to tell me.' She'd never met a trans person before, but she was so sweet about it. It was really nice to know that I didn't have to hold my breath anymore. That I could just be myself."*

AmeriCorps VISTA Sierra Barnes described a similar shift. At twenty-one, and just out of college, she served with Bridge Meadows, a multigenerational housing nonprofit in Oregon that supports foster families while providing older adults with affordable housing. The experience, she explained, changed her "views about the capacity of older adults and the value of aging." It also affected her thinking about public policies. "Working alongside older adults [...] opened my eyes to the inequity of our systems regarding age and the need for age-friendly initiatives across all sectors [...] I had never before considered how our cities aren't built for all ages. Sidewalks are cracked, making it enormously difficult for folks using walkers, canes, or wheelchairs to navigate our streets."†

Programs are strengthened by co-generational service because of combined skills and experience. Whether working in teams or as part of a cohort that engages together as a group, older and younger participants share knowledge and support each other's performance. This is what the American Association of Retired Persons (AARP) Senior Advisor Heather

---

* Sarah McKinney Gibson, "These AmeriCorps Members at SBP are Bridging the Generational Divide" Encore.org, December 3, 2020, https://encore.org/these-americorps-members-at-sbp-are-bridging-the-generational-divide/.

† Phyllis Segal. "Intergenerational National Service by, with, and for All Ages," *Ejournal of Public Affairs*, (June 2021): 6–8, http://www.ejournalofpublicaffairs.org/intergenerational-national-service-by-with-and-for-all-ages/.

Tinsley-Fix refers to as "knowledge spillover."*

Sherilyn Larkin, a sixty-six-year-old AmeriCorps/SBP member described how being part of an intergenerational service team in Puerto Rico meant "constantly learning each other's positions so we can all experience something different and support each other."† Retiree Charlene Young and recent college graduate Jordan Fong met through serving as Ameri-Corps literacy tutors with SSC's Reading Corps. Charlene and Jordan similarly described the valuable ways in which they were able to help each other.‡

Knowledge spillover also strengthened Colorado's COVID Containment Response Corps (CCRC), which mobilized an intergenerational mix of AmeriCorps members and Amer-iCorps Seniors RSVP volunteers. Intentionally connecting multiple generations was key to successfully contacting COVID-19 prospective cases within twenty-four hours and delivering 33,904 lab results to people tested by the state lab. Tech-savvy AmeriCorps NCCC members who were generally twenty-six and under helped AmeriCorps Seniors RSVP volunteers fifty-five and older navigate the technology needed to serve remotely. With that support, the RSVP volunteers were able to effectively reach 97 percent of their contact tracing calls. Kaira Esgate, CEO of America's Service Commissions

---

*   Heather Tinsley-Fix, "Three Reasons You Should Hire an Age-Diverse Work-force," American Association of Retired Persons, published August 20, 2020, https://www.aarp.org/work/employers/info-2020/age-diversity-value.html.

†   Sarah McKinney. Gibson, "These AmeriCorps members."

‡   Sarah McKinney Gibson, "In the Classroom or Over Zoom, These Tutors Created a Bond Across Generations," Encore.org, published February 26, 2021, https://encore.org/in-the-classroom-or-over-zoom-these-tutors-created-a-bond-across-generations/.

(who is also a contributing author in this book), points to this mix of AmeriCorps program funding streams and collaborating with state programs, as a "disruption-driven innovation" that created a highly diverse intergenerational corps to meet community needs.*

The value of co-generational service as standard practice also is seen in the business sector. Car manufacturer BMW found that age-diverse teams, combining the assets and experience of different generations, led to increased productivity.† A pilot project involving age-diverse work groups in health care, technology, and food manufacturing companies suggests that viewing "age-diversity as an asset rather than a deficit contributed to innovation."‡

Increased stability is another way that co-generational service strengthens programs. A Boston-area tutoring program, Generations Incorporated (recently renamed Literations), found that disruptive and costly turnover was reduced when older adult AmeriCorps members served alongside younger AmeriCorps VISTAs.§ According to SSC's Reading Corps director, Audrey Boland, including older adults in the corps brings

---

*   Kaira Esgate, "The Multifaceted Impacts of Service," in *Transforming Disruption into Impact.*

†   Christopher Loch et al, "The Globe: How BMW is Defusing the Demographic Time Bomb," Harvard Business Review, published March 2010, https://hbr.org/2010/03/the-globe-how-bmw-is-defusing-the-demographic-time-bomb.

‡   Marcie Pitt-Catsouphes et al., "Leveraging Age Diversity for Innovation," *Journal of Intergenerational Relationships* 11, no. 3 (2013): 238–254, https://www.tandfonline.com/doi/abs/10.1080/15350770.2013.810059.

§   Mary Gunn, "Efficiencies on the Road to a Multigenerational Workforce," Encore.org, published 2019, https://encore.org/wp-content/uploads/2019/06/EfficienciesontheRoadv9-1.pdf.

consistency to the relationship with the schools where they serve because older volunteers "tend to stay longer and serve multiple terms."[*]

Finally, tapping into more than one generation increases the number of potential volunteers. Recruitment strategies designed to attract the most participants focus on people who can make a meaningful commitment of time to service. This includes those who are young and have yet to take on the responsibilities that come with adulthood (such as jobs, career growth, parenting, and mortgages) and older adults as they move beyond midlife responsibilities and transition to an encore stage of life.

Even without the pandemic, demographic shifts make it compelling to connect the generations. For the first time, the United States has more people over sixty than under eighteen. In addition, as the country's White population grows older, the younger population is becoming increasingly diverse. In 2015, 22 percent of adults over sixty-five and 48 percent of youth were people of color, a gap that is likely to increase in upcoming decades.

Leaders can begin shifting to co-generational service through strategic recruitment. Age diversity in the Stockton Service Corps (SSC) resulted from the recruitment tactics used in one of the four programs operated by SSC partners. Most of the older corps members serve as tutors helping young children achieve grade-level reading and math proficiency. They were recruited through targeted outreach by the California Reading Corps to local churches, libraries, and community

---

[*]   Sarah McKinney Gibson, "In the classroom."

centers. By contrast, the other SSC partner programs recruit applicants through activities less likely to reach an older population, like internal program pipelines, university outreach events and career boards, and posting online through Service Year or student job boards like Handshake.

SSC members, ranging from their twenties to their sixties, serve individually rather than on teams. But SSC gathers them together for training and professional development. At one of these sessions, members talked about why young people were unable to access healthy food. Arielle Ayala, formerly the program's associate director, described how that meaningful interaction enabled participants to learn from and about each other:

"Katie, a service fellow in her twenties used words like 'food deserts' and 'redlining.' Carol, [who is] in her sixties, was unfamiliar with those terms. So, Katie described how access to healthy food is limited for many families as a result of housing policies that have relocated them to areas without access to basic resources. A light bulb went off for Carol. 'My family was forced to move around a lot,' she said. 'I didn't think about the consequences lasting this long. It still affects my students today.' A light bulb went off for Katie too. 'I didn't realize this had been happening for so long.'"

A light bulb went off for Arielle as well: Conversations like this, made possible by the intergenerational mix of service members, "could deliver more for our corps members than the traditional experience of resume building or career planning."

Research and shared learning among programs are needed to develop best practices for and increased understanding of co-generational service.

Bringing younger and older people together for the common purpose of meeting community needs obviously won't restore lives lost to COVID-19. But it can reduce the pandemic's impact on future generations and rebuild the social cohesion our democracy needs to thrive.

As the twenty-first century grapples with its unique challenges, it is time to disrupt age segregation.

Co-generational service is a good place to start.

Moving Beyond Transactional Volunteerism to Transformational Civic Engagement

Natalye Paquin

Natalye Paquin is the President and Chief Executive Officer at Points of Light. She is a visionary and results-oriented leader with a strong track record of performance and business transformation at high-paced organizations. Her work currently addresses civic engagement and volunteering, equity in the nonprofit space, and moving from purpose to action and outcomes in the business community. Previously, she held leadership positions at Girl Scouts of the USA and the Kimmel Center for Performing Arts in Philadelphia. Prior to that, she spent more than fifteen years in the education sector in legal and executive leadership roles. She began her career as an attorney, working as a civil rights attorney for the U.S. Department of Education, Office for Civil Rights.

* * *

"So, where do we see our organization in five years?"

It's a question many leaders have heard in organizational strategy planning sessions that start with a two-year, or five-year, or ten-year timetable.

I like to ask the question another way: *What's your team's moonshot for the difference you want to make?*

And, if you achieved it, what impact would it have on those around you, on your community? What would that feel like? What would you be experiencing?

With that picture in our minds, it's immediately clear what's important. Our priorities, plans, obstacles, must-dos—they all come into focus. That clarity allows us to determine how the disruptions that happen around us—and there will always be many—can become accelerants for the change we seek. Disruptions often expose the root issues in the systems we seek to change, creating an urgency we must convert to impact.

Real change comes, first, from believing it is possible and then having the focus and ambition to drive it. The will and drive to change is the antidote to inertia; it will challenge any forces that are comfortable with the status quo.

Points of Light, the organization that I lead, connects people, nonprofits, and corporations. We work together to drive change in communities and tackle society's toughest challenges. We give nonprofits the tools they need to be successful; we work with community-minded corporations to amplify their impact, and we empower millions of individual volunteers. And in our thirty-year history, we have never seen as much change as is happening right now.

In 2019, we began to talk with our partners about what we saw as the beginning of a new Civic Century. What we meant was that—more than ever before—people were becoming the driving force behind the changes in our world.

More People are Part of the Civic Circle

Technology was connecting people in new ways. Young people were using their voices more often (and more loudly). There was a new expectation that businesses should be forces for good. There were no longer any excuses for sitting on the sidelines—for anyone.

At the same time, we saw research that showed that while 30 percent of people volunteer, more than twice that number (62 percent) say they give back in other ways. To us, that meant that not only was the world changing; our role in it was changing too.

We could imagine a wave of sustained and meaningful civic engagement. We saw the energy. We knew we could help direct and channel it. We wanted to create a world where there were no barriers to civic engagement—where everyone sees, understands, and acts on their power to create change.

This was our moonshot. This was our idea of wild success.

So, we created a roadmap that would help people to engage with their communities and feel empowered to stand up and say, "I can help," beyond traditional, transactional volunteering.

We call it the Civic Circle. It's a framework that shows how we are surrounded—literally encircled—with opportunities for doing good and acting on causes we care about.

We can vote, we can volunteer, we can use our voices. We can donate, we can use our purchasing power and our social networks to get involved in making our communities better. We have an entire toolkit at our disposal, not just a single screwdriver.

The Civic Circle framework represents a vision *and* a strategy. The vision is for this kind of transformational civic engagement to become the norm; the strategy is about doing the work and creating opportunities at every point in the circle.

It was already happening—and then the disruptions of 2020 caused people to engage in new and different ways, beyond one-time, in-person volunteering, even more so than before. They moved from transactional engagements, like voting, to transformational actions like voting *and* registering others to vote or supporting a local campaign. The pandemic, a renewed focus on racial equity and social justice, and deepening and widening political divides put all of us in uncharted waters.

When in-person opportunities came to a halt in 2020, people were forced to deepen, expand, and adapt their engagement strategies. This is when we began to see people using their power to help others in new ways—delivering meals or groceries to the elderly, raising money for those who lost jobs or wages, donating to relief efforts, calling isolated individuals to provide comfort, and even participating in vaccine trials.

Of course, the same year, we saw political upheaval and protests against police brutality. We revisited conversations about racism and inherent bias in our systems and institutions. In 2021, we saw assaults on voting rights and on women's rights. People are engaging all around the Civic Circle, many of them for the very first time.

Nonprofits must be prepared for a shift from transactional, time-, and place-based volunteering to a comprehensive, transformative approach to engagement that is truly disruptive. While the systems we are trying to change are complex, society's issues are ultimately community issues—and we must approach them in more than one way. This is how change happens. The Civic Circle is your system for changing systems. How? By unlocking each person's civic power.

So, what does it mean?

So, why does it matter?

So, what do we do?

I love these questions.

First, the Civic Circle means civic action looks different. And activists look different too. We have people who have been doing this work for a long time. They understand the power of people and action. But there's a whole new generation of people coming into this space, and we need to learn from them to understand what actions matter.

Think about a young man, perhaps a member of Gen Z, whose first act of civic engagement was protesting the death of George Floyd. Today, maybe that young man has student loans, is underemployed or can't find a job or lost one in the pandemic. After experiencing the power of using his voice, do we expect him to sit idly by and wait for someone else to address these issues?

Points of Light research has shown that 67 percent of people like him participate in at least three different types of civic activities each year. Almost 80 percent of Gen Z has taken at least one action to address racial discrimination and inequality since May 2020. There's a whole new generation of power here;

it's not coming—it's *here*. Against this backdrop, businesses and nonprofits are going to have to adapt their approach to engagement.

What the social impact sector often values as effective might not be what's actually most influential.

Think of an election year, for example. You could solicit one person for a donation, which is great, but what if you leveraged their voice and that person is able to bring ten other people to the polls? While traditional actions are still critical, meeting people where they are in ways that feel exciting and authentic to them can lead to deeper engagement, thus accelerating change.

The Civic Circle matters because disruptions are going to keep happening. Whether these disruptions are climate-related, technology-related, or about persisting inequality—we know they will continue to occur. We also know people and organizations alike are going to continue to use their voices to drive the change they want to see in the world.

In June of 2020, according to Benevity Research, there was a staggering fifteen-fold increase in corporate donations to causes supporting social justice and racial equity. Benevity also found that there is a strong connection between individual giving and volunteering. If that's the case, is there a similar connection between, say, voting and activism, or between using your purchase power and stronger civic engagement?

Answering these types of questions will help organizations break down barriers and create new pathways for reaching individuals and empowering them to take action for causes they care about.

The Civic Circle is how we connect what we say we care about with what we do. For us at Points of Light, that meant looking at our role in providing tools, resources, and infra-structure that can stand the test of time for the nonprofit community.

The pandemic accelerated the need for this examination and caused us to act faster. We knew people needed new opportunities to engage, nonprofits needed new ways to deliver on their missions, and there were more community needs ranging from food insecurity to mental health.

Going Outside Your Comfort Zone

The racial reckoning also forced us to look at how we could unlock community assets, leverage our understanding of the nonprofit landscape, and use our tools to bring people together and bring visibility to important issues. We added Listen and Learn to our Civic Circle to encourage greater understanding among communities; understanding the root cause of issues and becoming educated before taking action is a critical step to engagement, and we wanted to be sure people understood that. We examined and addressed privilege in our Civic Life Today publication, and we used the power of our platform in ways we hadn't before by convening others in conversation through our Listen. Learn. Act to End Racism initiative.

Using our power in new ways is something we can all do.

I'm reminded of a gas station owner who noticed school children gathering behind his station to access his Wi-Fi. They needed the Wi-Fi to do homework and they didn't have internet access at home. So, he bought Wi-Fi boosters, set up tables and chairs, put up lights, and invited any student who needed Wi-Fi to come and do their work.

I'm reminded of a farmer in Kansas who connected farmers with people without food during the pandemic. He created an online community where farmers could get their produce to people in need. The group grew to one hundred forty thousand people nationwide, connecting thousands of hungry families with farmers who could help them.

Disruption is about going outside of our comfort zones. It's about doing what you can with what you have. And if you're not doing it, you're going to spend a lot of time doing work that isn't transformative. If you're always comfortable—if everybody around you is always comfortable—years will go by and nothing will change. You'll never start a dialogue, you'll never change the power dynamic, and you'll never know what you could have done.

Think about the amount of change that has occurred in just the last ten years. Could any amount of planning in 2011 have prepared us for the world we live in today? Not 2020, but *today*.

What will you do today? How will you continually change your approach consistently with the disruptions in the world? This isn't new and novel; it's necessary. It's the mindset we must have as we move forward in our Civic Century and harness the incredible, palpable wave of engagement that I believe is only just beginning.

So, what's your moonshot?

How will you use real, transformational civic engagement to get there?

And how amazing will it be once you've arrived?

Rethinking Strategy

Evolution of Corporate Volunteer Engagement

Jerome Tennille

Jerome Tennille is a Corporate Responsibility and Social Impact strategist who works in the hospitality industry and advises on volunteerism independently. His work focuses on designing, planning, and executing corporate employee volunteer programming to create positive social and environmental impact. He has expertise in bringing corporations and nonprofits together to build strategies that help advance long-term community goals and drive employee engagement. Prior to his work in corporate responsibility, he was the Senior Manager of Volunteer Services for Tragedy Assistance Program for Survivors (TAPS), a national nonprofit that serves military families experiencing loss. Jerome is also a social impact writer, and his work has been featured on *Impakter, Business 2 Community Magazine, VolunteerMatch, Nonprofit Information.com* and many other outlets. Jerome holds a master of sustainability leadership from Arizona State University and is designated as Certified in Volunteer Administration (CVA). Jerome is also a veteran of the U.S. Navy.

* * *

I often tell those interested in pursuing a career in Corporate Social Responsibility (CSR) to avoid spending thousands of dollars on a graduate-level certificate in CSR. I share this because whatever is taught during the certificate program will likely be outdated in the subsequent six to twelve months. You may find yourself with a certificate that looks good on paper but doesn't hold its long-term value.

Think about this example: If in December 2019 you earned a certificate in CSR, everything you know about CSR—philosophy, practices, language used in how the field talks about it—became nearly obsolete only months later with the onset of the COVID-19 pandemic, and later that summer with the murder of George Floyd. The emerging issues and tactics used to address these issues are outpacing academic curriculum. The way companies understand their role in solving some of the world's most critical issues has changed dramatically. In my estimation, CSR—including corporate employee volunteering—has advanced many years in just the span of months. While driven out of necessity, we are turning a page in how companies operate responsibly through the act of service. I never would have predicted how short a time it took to set this evolution in motion.

It was July 2018, and I was planning the following year's company-wide day of service for our corporate headquarters. When you're engaging thousands of employees in a single day, it requires deep thought, intention, and careful programming that takes nearly a year to plan.

Having gone through my after-action report just months

prior, it was clear there were opportunities to diversify the types of volunteer opportunities we offered employees, one of which was virtual volunteerism. But before I continue, let's level set. Virtual volunteerism isn't new. In fact, virtual forms of service have been around for about three decades. But even in the year 2018, the world was, in many ways, still not ready to fully embrace virtual service. I recall introducing the option back then, only to be met with a salvo of questions—understandably so. I'll admit that in the face of many of these questions, even with many attempts to paint a picture of what virtual volunteering looks like, I often fell short because that "picture" often looks like a person sitting at a computer. And while my descriptions of the service and outcomes were likely accurate, perhaps my descriptions never felt as tangible or impactful as the physical, face-to-face act of volunteer engagement.

While virtual volunteering wasn't unheard of, I didn't immediately realize that the idea at the time may not have been fully understood, and therefore may have been largely considered ineffective or underestimated by those for whom the concept was less familiar. Unless you've actually done it, virtual volunteering can be a hard concept to wrap one's head around. The other reason there seemed to be a "disconnect" with virtual volunteering is due to our deep, innate desire for human-to-human interaction. We have learned so much about corporate volunteer engagement since then; this accumulated knowledge can (and should) be practiced and applied today.

You see, employee volunteering is one of many tools that can achieve a company's CSR goals. Of course, the primary goal is to engage company employees to support the communities where that company does business. But this engagement has additional positive outcomes, like injecting purpose into the employee experience, adding to a positive organizational culture, and even supporting or amplifying a brand's reputation. Perhaps virtual volunteering broke the mold of what one would consider effective employee engagement in 2018, just as remote work was once frowned upon at many companies.

I want to be clear—there's nothing wrong with engaging in volunteerism to satisfy the objectives of increasing employee engagement and building brand reputation. I'd even say those objectives are incredibly necessary. I submit to you that society has generally sought group activities that had a tangible outcome, one you (or the employees) can touch.

In mid-2018, we chose to forgo adding virtual volunteering to our 2019 day of service. Why? Because there needed to be a convergence of several critical elements that never came together; at that particular time, the necessary ingredients just didn't exist.

Fast forward to late 2019, I once again sought to include virtual volunteerism into the programming for our upcoming mid-2020 day of service. What I didn't know at the time was that the world would change in a way that would forever unlock creativity and open-mindedness in how companies respond to crisis. In many ways, for the better.

The Shift in Mindset Within CSR

In 2020, the world was engulfed in crisis after crisis. When the pandemic took a turn for the worse in the spring of 2020, everything came to a sudden, grinding halt; the programming for our 2020 community day of service, the rebrand and launching of new programming, *all* of it stopped. Then with the murder of George Floyd came a sweeping self-reckoning of major institutions as the country grappled yet again with racial injustice.

These two events mandated drastic change across all aspects of life, rightfully so. They required a recognition that the mechanisms of change that got us to this point were no longer effective for creating the positive momentum we want to see moving forward.

Society at large became wildly open to new ideas, rising to the occasion.

There was a shift in mindset that provided the path for adopting new practices to create change. In many ways, this change is reflected in how companies engage in serving their communities. For example, the virtual volunteerism that I proposed in 2018 (and later in 2019) automatically became the expected norm during the pandemic. Sure, this "new norm" evolved out of necessity, but the pandemic became the catalyst for companies to begin reimagining the role virtual engagement would play in their CSR programs.

In the wake of George Floyd's murder, when so many employees felt unseen and unheard, companies more clearly understood the vital importance of giving voice to their employees. What evolved was a formal acknowledgment of informal mechanisms of change. As a result, some companies began to fully recognize grassroots advocacy.

Even in the aftermath of the economic crisis that unfolded because of the pandemic, many companies continued their volunteer efforts, deepening their current partnerships—while taking on new ones—and focusing on what made the most sense for their communities, their employees, and their brand.

Some companies even chose to forgo partnerships with associations and membership-based groups, whether out of financial necessity or due to the newly realized value in investing in their own in-house CSR expertise.

Adoption of New Tactics, Techniques, and Procedures

As businesses implemented remote work protocols, they also had to adjust their employee volunteer programs; in fact, many of these adjustments remain today. Naturally, virtual and socially distanced forms of volunteering became an equalizer that allowed companies to engage their employees while still enforcing work-from-home mandates. Some companies ceased all in-person volunteering, moving their volunteer engagement fully online by creating, planning, and executing virtual opportunities with their partners. Others chose to engage in hybrid forms of service. We, too, more actively introduced virtual and hybrid forms of service. We very thoughtfully researched and curated volunteer opportunities—some with current partners and others with new ones—and created toolkits to focus on empowering and equipping employees in their respective markets. While this may have quickly become the norm for many companies, others adopted different tactics.

One tactic that proved powerful—yet which was taken by only a few companies—was recognizing informal volunteerism. Although many don't think of peaceful protesting, marching, and other grassroots advocacy as volunteering, *it is*. It's an informal mechanism to support a specific cause or group of people or to change the tide of social and environmental norms by trying to influence large-scale policy through the gift of one's time.

Similar to how some companies give Paid Volunteer Time Off (PTVO) to employees who want to volunteer, some companies—like Washington State-based software company Icertis and &pizza, the American fast casual pizza restaurant chain—allowed what's been coined Paid Social Justice Time Off (PSJTO) for employees who wanted to participate in peaceful protesting in the wake of George Floyd's death. This is informal volunteering. These actions are peer-to-peer through grassroots advocacy, families helping their loved ones and friends directly, and communities galvanizing to support each other directly while circumventing the formal constraints of large tax-exempt institutions.

What's not so well-known is that 70 percent of the world's volunteerism is informal.

This isn't a new tactic. Patagonia, the popular outdoor clothing retailer, has been doing this for some time in their quest for environmental justice. But what *is* new is the shift in mindset that's allowing companies to actively create mechanisms for employees to volunteer for causes they care about. It's a sure sign that the boundaries and the very definition of CSR have changed forever.

Since 2020, companies have become much more thoughtful about how they serve communities. 2020 and early 2021 provided companies a moment for self-reckoning about who they support, how they're providing that support, and their role in advancing social issues with more authenticity, greater purpose, more intentional programming, and perhaps even greater brand influence.

All of these ongoing efforts require companies to have the subject matter expertise in-house.

Businesses Recognize CSR as a "Must Have" In-House Expertise

Society's demand for companies to act responsibly in 2020 through 2021 gave rise to companies re-exploring their own CSR subject matter expertise beyond the traditional business functions. This led to not just a hiring boom, but also to what some would call an Environmental, Social, and Governance (ESG) talent shortage.

But there is a cost to companies that rely on their own in-house CSR practitioners, as those companies often drop their memberships to the associations and membership-based organizations. In some instances, organizations that have built their brand based on providing expertise in ESG services through benchmarking services and peer-based conversations have had to rethink their value proposition. This of course is in part because companies are now developing related subject matter expertise internally.

For companies feeling the greatest financial strain due to the economic downturn caused by the pandemic, out of necessity they've tended to jettison their fee-based memberships. Many of these membership-based organizations charge thousands of dollars annually—or in some cases tens of thousands—for access to resources, volunteerism toolkits, benchmarking studies and other "best practices" to support CSR programs.

Many of these same memberships convened peer-based discussion.

But in many ways, the new reliance on digital media created opportunities for CSR practitioners to seek their own networking opportunities through LinkedIn and other social media platforms, which in turn made some membership benefits—namely peer-to-peer networking—obsolete. No longer do CSR practitioners need to connect in-person or virtually through an association. They can simply send a LinkedIn request to schedule time for informational interviews on relevant topics, completely bypassing large convening organizations that would otherwise charge a hefty fee to facilitate the connection.

As companies and CSR practitioners become less reliant on membership-based organizations, there are more opportunities to spend that membership-fee on other programmatic areas and with organizations on the frontline engaged in direct service.

The Future Favors Bold Corporate Action

There's a saying I love: "Fortune favors the bold." I have seen firsthand how facing challenges with steadfast determination, courage, and bold, decisive action leads to success.

When addressing social and environmental issues in the communities where we do business, I say take the same tactic. Here's how:

Reintroduce the Big, Hairy, Audacious Goal (BHAG)

Just as those across the globe have adopted new ideas that were previously considered too extreme to address new and emerging issues, we must continue to seek out other BHAGs that may have been shelved in the past.

Be bold. Just as it took a pandemic to make virtual volunteering the expected norm, now is the time to reintroduce other ideas. Many people are desperate for change because they've recognized the systems that got us here will no longer work to create the transformational change we're seeking. This, too, applies to how we engage volunteers. While virtual and hybrid forms of volunteering will never be a primary driver of how critical issues are solved, they're here to stay.

Recognize Informal Mechanisms of Volunteering

As we think about giving voice to our employees, we must give them greater agency in the nonprofits they choose to serve when formally volunteering. But we must also recognize the contributions to their communities through informal peer-to-peer actions. This could be accomplished through the introduction of PSJTO. Remember, 70 percent of the world's volunteering is peer-to-peer outside the structures of formalized institutions, and PSJTO may be an effective way to honor that. While adopting PSJTO may not be appropriate for all companies, there are certainly ways to recognize other forms of peer-to-peer volunteering.

Invest in True In-House CSR Expertise

ESG issues are becoming increasingly important to corporations and their stakeholders, so allocating the necessary resources to hire qualified subject matter experts dedicated to supporting CSR would be a wise investment for companies. Using myself as an example, when I started my role in CSR in

2017, I was charged with helping the company achieve the goal of fifteen million hours of volunteer service by the year 2025. I believe I was selected because of my expertise in volunteerism. And while this was a pre-COVID decision, it's becoming the expected norm for companies in how they invest in their CSR efforts. That theme is also what's fueling a change in how companies engage with membership-based organizations.

While membership-based organizations will always play a role in advancing CSR and corporate volunteerism practices, it is now a necessity—long past due—for companies to hire CSR professionals just as they do traditional business functions.

Today, consumers are using their purchasing power to buy goods and services they believe align with their whole person. They're seeking to work for employers and brands that live their core values. The landscape of CSR and how companies understand their role in solving critical issues has been accelerated by many years.

Companies that don't adopt big, brave, bold practices will risk being left behind.

Why We Invest in Volunteerism: A Funder's Perspective

Rina Cohen

Rina Cohen works at UJA-Federation of New York where she leads the organization's strategic volunteerism grant portfolio. To date, she has helped steward more than ten million dollars in grants to build volunteer infrastructure at over thirty nonprofit agencies. Additionally, Rina manages UJA's unrestricted funding application process to UJA's sixty core partners, totaling thirty-four million dollars in communal investments. Rina was a key member of several special initiatives including UJA's COVID-19 Vaccine Education & Access and Census 2020 teams, where she was responsible for designing and realizing the grant process for community-based organizations. Rina completed her master's in nonprofit management at the Wagner School of Public Service at NYU and bachelor's degree at Barnard College.

* * *

It is September 2019, and as part of my role as a grants manager supporting UJA-Federation of New York's antipoverty agenda, I am visiting United Jewish Council (UJC) of the Lower East Side to meet with UJC's Executive Director, Betsy Jacobson. When she hurries in, out of breath, wearing her signature high heels, it's clear she has something important to share.

Betsy gets straight to the point: "I don't have enough people-power. We're at our breaking point."

UJC is a small and mighty fifty-year-old social service organization serving a diverse community of mainly working poor and older adults. It is preparing to launch a new digital food pantry system.

Funded by UJA, the digital system enables clients to access food in the most dignified way; once logged into the system, clients see the pantry's available inventory and can select the foods they want. Their customized bags are either picked up at the food pantry or delivered to their homes at a selected time. This model reduces lines, wait times, and food waste. It also enables clients to choose food that aligns with their needs, preferences, and dietary practices.

While the digital pantry has many advantages over traditional models, it requires more people to operate efficiently. UJC simply does not have enough staff or volunteers to fill all needed roles. Additional people are needed to help clients place online orders, pack custom orders, and deliver packages. This is in stark contrast to the way UJC's pantry operated for years; clients used to submit their orders on paper, in person, during select hours of the week. And then they waited. The process was time-consuming for clients and the limited hours posed barriers for older adults and working families.

On this September morning, I have invited Beth Steinhorn, President of VQ Volunteer Strategies and a volunteer engagement consultant, to join the meeting to assess whether volunteers can serve as a solution as the system transitions. With clients soon arriving to place orders, Betsy quickly takes us to the food pantry where we find a busy part-time paid intern stocking food items and updating inventory using pen and paper. Boxes and papers are flying. With no steady volunteers supporting the pantry, it's all hands on deck—including Betsy in her high heels. This approach is not sustainable, and we all recognize that with the transition to the digital system, Betsy and her team will need even more hands and a different method of organizing.

Beth and I believe that volunteers can help the UJC team meet the growing client demand and deliver food directly to clients through the digital platform. We invite UJC to join two other digital pantries in the Volunteer Accelerator, UJA's new initiative to expand or enhance a specific program through volunteers. Teams from each pantry will receive support from VQ Volunteer Strategies on how to professionally engage volunteers—from recruitment and screening to onboarding and retention. Without hesitating, Betsy agrees to participate.

Training and coaching under the Volunteer Accelerator launched in November 2019, and teams began building their volunteer program from the ground up, redesigning websites for online recruitment, creating volunteer handbooks, and instituting screening protocols.

And then COVID hit.

COVID posed a whole new set of challenges—a twofold increase in clients experiencing food insecurity at UJC and an in-person pantry model that needed to become remote. During COVID, clients could not pick up food packages. Our timing for the Volunteer Accelerator was serendipitous, yet the work we expected to take a year needed to happen over-night. In April 2020, UJC put their volunteer plans into action, delivering an unprecedented four hundred Passover packages to clients' homes with the help of brave and committed volunteers. This was just the beginning.

UJC's expertise in recruiting and engaging volunteers was growing, but so was the demand for food. To keep up, UJC needed funds—funds for more food, funds for a van to deliver the packages, and funds to hire a volunteer engagement professional to manage the program. UJA provided support and by July 2020, UJC was the go-to organization serving Kosher food needs on the Lower East Side.

Training UJC on how to professionally engage volunteers allowed them to significantly increase the number of clients served and meals delivered. Before UJA intervened with support, UJC served forty-five hundred meals in person to 627 unique clients without any volunteers. Thanks, in large part, to the assistance of eighty-one volunteers, in Fiscal Year 2020,* UJC served 31,014 meals to 1,182 unique clients. In fiscal year 2021,† UJC continued to increase the food program,

---

* UJC's and UJA's fiscal years run July through June, so Fiscal Year 2020 ran July 1, 2019, through June 30, 2020.
† UJC's and UJA's fiscal years run July through June, so Fiscal Year 2021 ran July 1, 2020, through June 30, 2021.

engaging one hundred and ten volunteers to help pack and deliver nearly forty thousand meals.

Every time that UJA helps another pantry adopt the digital ordering system, we see the same effect: number of clients served increases because barriers are lowered. One can order online from any location, any time of day. However, organizations cannot grow their pantry without enough people to train clients on technology, and to package and deliver food. As paid staff is not an option in most cases, a sophisticated volunteer strategy is needed to optimize this digital system.

In less than two years, UJC expanded its volunteer program into other areas of the organization, beyond the pantry. In Fiscal Year 2021, they engaged 264 volunteers in both the digital pantry and a variety of other services. That same year, Bloomberg Foundation, in partnership with UJA, selected UJC to be one of its go-to organizations for corporate volunteerism. Since then, Bloomberg employees made over three hundred fifty caring calls to UJC's clients to check-in and provide companionship.

A formal evaluation showed that all three digital food pantries in the Volunteer Accelerator measurably improved their use of volunteer engagement best practices (recruiting, screening, training, and tracking volunteers) and significantly increased the number of food pantry volunteers. Two of the three increased the number of remote clients accessing the pantry and receiving home-delivered meals by tenfold. As we hypothesized, organizations began to use volunteers within a range of programs, not just food assistance.

Another Accelerator participant, JCC of the Rockaway Peninsula, engaged more than seventy-five virtual volunteers in the

2020 Census project and one hundred volunteers in a "Get out the Vote" campaign, also mobilizing volunteers to support the needs of Holocaust survivors and older adults in the COVID vaccine process. Without having participated in the Accelerator, these organizations would not have known how to effectively engage volunteers for these purposes.

Building on the Volunteer Accelerator

In September 2020, recognizing the increased demand for employment services due to pandemic-related unemployment, UJA committed to helping organizations enhance employment services. Building on the success of the Volunteer Accelerator, UJA invited three organizations to participate in the second Volunteer Accelerator, this time focusing on engaging volunteers to build their capacity to help clients find jobs. When UJA called the organizations to discuss joining this Accelerator, one organization shared that they rely on one or two staff members to review the resumes of hundreds of clients.

While staff were able to assist a significant number of clients, we speculated that the experience and outcome could be even greater if volunteers with industry-specific expertise reviewed the resumes instead. During the height of the pandemic, many professionals of all ages were home with flexible schedules and time to give, while staff at these agencies were stretched beyond capacity. Through this Accelerator, organizations learned how to engage experienced volunteers to mentor and coach clients on interviewing and resume-writing and to support client networking.

While the program models are similar, each organization leveraged the cultural expertise of its volunteers to meet the unique needs of those seeking employment. As an example, Marks JCH of Bensonhurst, a community center serving a predominantly Russian-speaking population, provided twenty-five English language learners with opportunities to practice workplace-related conversational English in on-going volunteer-led groups. All participants reported feeling more confident during practice interviews and more excited about their next steps to employment.

In March 2021, recognizing that social isolation among older adults was intensifying, UJA sought to help organizations expand older adult services. At the time, a UJA survey found that 28 percent of our partner agencies were having trouble reaching their older adult clients. Organizations did not have enough people or time to connect with members on an on-going basis. We reasoned that they could reach additional older adults through the support of volunteers.

Two agencies with a proven track record of supporting older adults were invited to participate in our third Volunteer Accelerator, each receiving coaching, training, and funding to hire volunteer engagement staff. To facilitate the task of reaching older adults in their homes, volunteers were engaged to make caring calls, train older adults on technology, deliver essential items, and offer virtual programming. In the six months since beginning the Volunteer Accelerator, one participant, Suffolk Y, added 153 new volunteers; twenty of these volunteers were older adults who led weekly classes and social clubs, engaging one hundred of their peers a week in conversations ranging from American History to dating in a new world. Volunteers extend the reach of the organizations, and most importantly, create meaningful connections and social experiences for those who are most isolated.

The Accelerator model was built on UJA's seven-year investment in helping organizations develop capacity to meet critical needs through volunteerism, an investment totaling more than ten million dollars, supporting over thirty organizations. Prior to the Accelerator, UJA helped to enhance volunteer engagement by training and certifying fourteen organizations as "Service Enterprises" through a national program that helps organizations embrace volunteer engagement as a core strategy.

The Accelerator was designed to integrate volunteers into a specific program or service. It costs UJA approximately five thousand dollars to coach each organization on how to strategically engage volunteers through the Volunteer Accelerator. Organizations are then invited to apply for a volunteer program grant ranging from forty-five to eighty thousand dollars a year for up to five years. These are small investments with significant impacts that we have been able to document.

Return on Investment

In 2021, UJA invested $1.3 million in volunteer programs supporting fourteen organizations. These grants were used for volunteer engagement professionals' salaries and other related expenses such as software and volunteer engagement training. On average, UJA's investment represents 70 percent of total volunteer program expenses. These organizations mobilized volunteers for a total of 124,598 hours. Using Independent

Sector's value of $33.17 for a volunteer hour in New York,* these volunteer contributions are equivalent to $4.1 million, a three-fold return on investment for every UJA dollar spent! Viewed through the lens of staffing, these 124,598 hours translate to the work of sixty full-time employees. As funders, these numbers demonstrate the return on our investments and help our nonprofit partners share the impact of volunteers with donors, staff, and their boards. We recognize that volunteers do not replace paid staff; however, in many cases, they can extend and expand the organization's capacity. While these numbers are compelling, they do not capture the social, emotional, and spiritual impact that volunteers have on the people and organizations they serve, nor does this illustrate the impact that our investment has had on the volunteers themselves.

Crisis Preparedness

While we did not expect the COVID-19 pandemic, we were prepared for it. We helped establish strong volunteer departments across our partner organizations and knew we could rely on them to serve their communities when the pandemic hit. Organizations that were most nimble and adaptable were those that had volunteers woven into the fabric of their organizations. People wanted to do good, and our partner organizations had the tools and a sound infrastructure in place to deploy volunteers to meet emerging needs. These partners mobilized volunteers to deliver food, personal protective

---

* Independent Sector, "Value of Volunteer Time by State," https://independentsector.org/wp-content/uploads/2018/04/Value-of-Volunteer-Time-by-State-2001-2020.pdf.

equipment, and other critical supplies. Volunteers checked in with their community's most vulnerable members and offered virtual programs for those at home. When the vaccine became available, volunteers assisted older adults and those who faced technology or language barriers with accessing appointments. Months later, when Hurricane Ida hit, the same volunteers helped clean up local institutions.

A strong and diverse volunteer base can be mobilized to meet a variety of communal needs when managed effectively. Unfortunately, the COVID-19 pandemic will not be the last crisis that our partner organizations experience, and forward-thinking organizations will continue to invest in volunteers to meet needs that they cannot yet anticipate.

Build Caring Communities

UJA is a Jewish organization that believes in the power of acts of *hesed* (the Hebrew term for loving-kindness) to create communities that are caring, connected, resilient, and self-sustaining. By investing in volunteer infrastructure, we empower communities to respond to the unique needs of their community members through volunteers. Volunteers can offer compassion, time, and attention to a neighbor or stranger in need; they have the power to lift a person from a place of despair to a place of hope.

We also know that volunteers themselves benefit through the act of giving. In Rabbi Jonathan Sacks's book, *To Heal a Fractured World*,* he writes, "The paradox of altruism is that

---

* Jonathan Sacks, *To Heal a Fractured World: The Ethics of Responsibility*, (London: Bloomsbury Academic, 2013): 270.

the hope we give to others returns to us undiminished and enlarged. All I know is that the greatest achievement in life is to have been, for one other person, even for one moment, an agent of hope."

UJA continues to invest in volunteer engagement not only because it transforms organizations by helping them reach more people more effectively, but also because we believe acts of kindness transform individuals who, in turn, transform communities for the better.

All Together: Volunteers and Staff Pull in the Same Direction to Achieve Results

Lauren Spero and Cyndi Zagieboylo

Lauren Spero is the National Multiple Sclerosis (MS) Society's Vice President of Volunteer & Community Engagement. Lauren leads the organization's effort to implement strategic volunteer engagement and leverage the talent of over fifty thousand volunteers annually. She oversees a team of volunteer engagement professionals who build relationships with volunteers to ensure they contribute at their highest potential and feel empowered, invested, and committed. Lauren also serves on the National Alliance for Volunteer Engagement Leadership Team. Prior to working for the Society, Lauren led a service-learning program at a university and staffed an interagency council on homelessness and affordable housing for the state of Ohio.

Cyndi Zagieboylo began her career at the National Multiple Sclerosis Society in 1985 and has worked with every CEO of the organization, including founder Sylvia Lawry. In 2011, Cyndi became president and CEO of the Society, noting that achieving the organization's mission is her life's work. As CEO and president, Cyndi serves on the Society's National Board of Directors, on the MS International Federation Board of Trustees, and on the Board of Directors for Research!America. Cyndi is an avid supporter of volunteer engagement efforts and fully embraces her role as "Chief Engagement Officer." Born in Norfolk, Massachusetts, Cyndi received her bachelor's degree in rehabilitation counseling and psychology from Springfield College, and master's degree in social psychology from the University of Connecticut.

The National MS Society's investment in strategic volunteer engagement is led by our President & CEO, Cyndi Zagieboylo, in partnership with Lauren Spero, Vice President, Volunteer & Community Engagement. Lauren's role is to lead a team of volunteer engagement professionals that ensure all our volunteer practices are culturally aligned and implemented throughout the organization. Given this unique approach and partnership, this chapter is written from the CEO's perspective, but coauthored by Lauren and Cyndi.

* * *

A few years back—pre-COVID-19—a teacher friend of mine told me a story about a grade school field day competition among her students. The teams had formed organically, and one team clearly had all the advantages that come with weight and confidence—the competition was tug-of-war. Rather than intervening to even out the teams in a rational, athletic-based way, my friend instead gravitated to the underweight team. She called out to them, "Okay team, let's huddle!" The children quickly gathered and put their heads together, quite literally, while my friend explained the strategy to winning tug-of-war.

She told them, "Hold the rope with both hands, start with your left foot in front. At the sound of the bell—all together—lean back and pull. Keep both feet on the ground and both hands gripping the rope; use all your weight, lean back—all together."

After the game was over and the lighter, less confident team had won, she overheard two of the kids saying, "You beat us like it was nothing!"

The winning team member replied, "Next time, you should try a huddle."

I often reflect on this story and the lessons it can teach us as we drive strategy. To me, it shows the power of communication, leveraging all our resources, and pulling—all together—in the same direction. These concepts were key to the National Multiple Sclerosis Society's success as we refocused our volunteer engagement to navigate the pandemic.

As the Chief Executive Officer, one of my responsibilities is to set the organizational culture in partnership with the Chair of the National Board of Directors, a position that transitions every two to four years in our organization. The teamwork between those top positions is reflected throughout all layers of volunteers and staff.

Role clarity and effective communication along with a culture of teamwork and collegiality enable us to pivot quickly, get set, and all pull in the same direction. We "huddle" to establish goals and roles, we provide clear calls to action, and we leverage individual strengths to achieve the outcomes desired.

The National MS Society engages over fifty thousand volunteers annually. Volunteer partners are involved in every aspect of our work, including over eight hundred trustees who serve on local boards across the country; one thousand self-help group leaders who provide a place for connection; dozens of administrative volunteers who join us in the office; thousands of event volunteers who ensure exceptional event experiences; Advisory Committees who provide informed, consensus advice to the CEO; and thousands of activists who advocate at both state and federal levels for issues important to the MS community. Building relationships and clearly establishing what we are going for in all our activities are at the heart of our volunteer engagement strategy.

Assembling Our Team: Staying Connected until We Can Be Together Again

In many circumstances, an outsider cannot differentiate between a volunteer and a staff member. CEO Advisory Committees are a good example of this collegiality playing out. Members of committees are nominated and selected based on their competencies and expertise to accomplish specific work or answer certain questions—deemed important from the CEO's perspective. They participate in committee work as equals, without titles. We define the work, designate a leader, and are clear about team member roles. There is a career path for those seeking leadership opportunities. The success of our volunteer strategy is predicated on an established culture, which is set by the CEO, and staff initiative to know and engage volunteers, having mutually respectful relationships and being deeply connected through the outcome we collectively desire.

Beginning in 2020, the COVID-19 pandemic disrupted our work. We needed to make sure it did not disrupt our relationships. For us, connecting in person at conferences, meetings, and at over six hundred fundraising events each year was critical to building relationships. These gatherings provide a connection point and shared experience that deepen trust and commitment. Like the rest of the world, the way we conducted business drastically changed in March 2020. All fundraising events were postponed or moved to a virtual format, meetings were canceled, and travel stalled out; we were left missing the opportunity to connect face-to-face with a huge segment of our workforce—volunteers.

Understanding the importance of maintaining connections, we adopted a new strategy: to stay connected until we could be together again. Staff checked in with their team of volunteer partners to maintain open lines of communication. Accustomed to calling a few times a year with an ask for time or talent, staff shifted to check on personal wellness and then on volunteer aspirations and career paths. We took the time to connect with volunteers to understand how they saw themselves involved with the organization in the future. We explored ways we could engage volunteers in new, deeper ways.

The Huddle

As challenges cropped up, we assembled the right teams of volunteers to help us address the issues at hand. We regularly huddled with individuals and groups to solve problems and address challenges in the moment.

For example, our National Medical Advisory Committee, a

group of top medical experts in the MS field from across the country and experienced staff, developed information and guidance for people with MS to respond to the reality of the pandemic. As we began to understand more about COVID-19, we brought this volunteer group together to respond to the questions on people's minds—questions, for example, concerning whether this virus is more dangerous for people with MS, if MS medications interact with COVID, and whether a COVID vaccine is safe for people with MS. The National Medical Advisory Committee was regularly convened, studied all available evidence, and developed guidance throughout the pandemic to populate the Society's COVID-19 webpage and to transmit in a newly launched, weekly *Ask an MS Expert* webinar series.

As CEO, my priority was the eight hundred plus trustees, directors, advisory committee members—including the aforementioned National Medical Advisory Committee—, and our leadership volunteers who are spread throughout communities across the country. We had an established Board Portal with a usage growing to our 100 percent quarterly access goal. Effective use of this communication technology allowed us to provide weekly email updates during the messiest part of the pandemic. Ensuring transparency throughout the hardest decision-making processes while describing leadership expectations was critical to maintaining confidence and gaining support. I was able to communicate important updates, calls to action, and specific talking points about decisions made. Messages were timely, relevant, and followed a predictable cadence. Leadership volunteers knew how and what decisions were being made, what they could do to be supportive, and how they could provide input.

I continue to huddle regularly with volunteer groups and key leaders as we learn more about what our future looks like and the work that lies ahead. Volunteer engagement staff and other staff across the organization huddle with their volunteer networks to move important priorities forward. Assembling the right team of volunteer leaders for shared problem solving continues to be a highly effective strategy as we navigate a rapidly changing world.

Pulling in the Same Direction

Early on, we realized our world was forever changed. Holding onto prepandemic ways or waiting until we could "get back to normal" was not an option. We need to keep our eye on the future, be adaptable, and make sure everyone on our team is pulling in the same direction. We know from previous experience that if people don't hear from you, they'll assume nothing is happening. Overcommunicating became the norm.

To make these adjustments, we leaned into our relationship-building strategy. My first communication related to the pandemic was sent on March 17, 2020. That email, and the weekly emails that followed, included MS Society news, updates, and changes related to our business operations, including decisions we needed volunteer leaders to be aware of such as event cancellations or postponements and organizational restructuring decisions that included reduced staffing.

As the pandemic persisted, decisions on how we planned to ramp up to in-person gatherings were added to our communications. At the same time, agendas for boards of trustees and advisory committees reinforced these messages. Open calls for leadership volunteers provided opportunities for a real time exchange with the CEO, National Board of Director Chair, and other key NMS leaders.

In the early days of the pandemic, the most common question we got from volunteer leaders was "What can I do to help?" This essential question underscored the importance of including a clear call to action in all communications. There was no better time to capitalize on this genuine offer of support than in the moment. So, we had an answer and a place to direct interest and enthusiasm.

Some of the calls to action for our volunteers were small but impactful, such as sharing information about MS and COVID with their network or bolstering our fundraising efforts by increasing awareness about virtual events or our COVID-19 Response Fund. Other times, we made big asks, like the National Medical Advisory Committee work to ensure people affected by MS had informed answers to their questions. Regardless of the magnitude of the ask, we found that people responded best when we were clear about what they could do to support us through the disruption brought on by the pandemic.

The pandemic brought to the surface and in the media greater awareness of racial disparities and racism, which warranted public proclamations on behalf of our organization. Our leadership volunteer communication pattern was well established by the time of our social media proclamation describing our antiracism stance and actions. Communicating with volunteer leaders ahead of public communications is a clear demonstration of the respect we have for them, and it prepares them to respond effectively with consistent message points. This is especially important when moving through challenging times which can include social unrest and political polarization.

Relationship Management and Engagement is Essential Now and for the Future

Volunteers are integral to our ability to navigate a landscape full of unknowns, and we need strong relationship management strategies to mobilize this resource. MS Society volunteers are an extension of staff, and the pandemic provided an opportunity to lean into that reality. Moving forward, we need volunteers to continue leading *with* us—ensuring that communities across the country know the Society is here to be a conduit for people with MS to get what they need, to leverage their expertise and connections to help us provide timely and relevant information and resources to people affected by MS, and to maintain a direct line of communication to connect people with each other and resources in meaningful ways.

Our future success as an organization will hinge on our ability to carry these lessons through the pandemic and beyond:

1. **Prioritize relationship management.** We will continue to be disciplined about staying connected to volunteers so they are ready to engage when the time is right. We will plan for relationship management, whether that's regularly checking in to see how volunteers are navigating the world in which we are living, planning virtual gatherings so volunteers can network with others and draw from shared inspiration and passion,

or starting conversations about volunteer career paths and engagement journeys with the organization. Our volunteer engagement team will continue to develop and implement relationship management strategies, including volunteer career paths and a pipeline, to ensure we have the volunteer force we need to support our organization of tomorrow.

2. **Ensure effective communication in every engagement strategy**. If people don't hear from you, they may assume nothing is happening and their questions and expressions of anxiety can feel frustrating. I will continue our regularly cadenced emails to leadership volunteers that we initiated during the pandemic. Our formula for success will continue to be (1) provide regular updates, (2) celebrate successes, and (3) offer calls to action.

3. **Build a culture of volunteer engagement and live by it.** Engagement and relationship building is a central role for every nonprofit President & CEO. There is no way we could staff up to accomplish all we do, and it wouldn't be as effective or authentic even if we could.

We are a movement by and for people affected by MS. People affected by MS and volunteers must have trust and confidence in the leadership and the organization. We need them to share that feeling of trust with others—that's powerful. For our leadership volunteers, building community trust and confidence is a priority. With over eight hundred community leaders spread throughout the country partnering with local staff leaders, we have powerful presence—a national organization with local community presence. It's so important. The CEO is the face of the organization and people can tell that your heart is in it.

With trust, people will embrace and amplify your messages; with trust, they will provide feedback and support. When you share your concerns and challenges, showing some vulnerability, they will rally. Let volunteers know what you need from them. Volunteer engagement must be a year-round, consistent part of your role. Embrace it! A coordinated volunteer engagement strategy for the entire organization ensures a supportive culture in good times and during a pandemic, or whatever comes. I'm so grateful for our volunteer partners. Together, we will transform the pandemic's greatest disruptions into opportunities for success and growth as we all move toward a world free of MS.

As tug-of-war taught those students on that sunny afternoon, individual efforts alone won't guarantee success. But communication, teamwork, and coordinated strategy to pull in the same direction can make any organization—no matter the size—move through disruptions in the right direction.

Disruptions Move Skills-Based Volunteering into Mainstream

Danielle Holly

Danielle Holly is currently leading learning programs at The Aspen Institute Business & Society Program. Until 2022, Danielle was the CEO of Common Impact, a national nonprofit that connects individuals, companies, and social change organizations in skills-based volunteer programs that are designed to fight inequality. She is a contributing writer to Nonprofit Quarterly, the Stanford Social Innovation Review, and other industry publications on the importance of civic engagement and transforming service into a strategic resource for our communities. She hosts the Pro Bono Perspectives podcast, which lifts up the voices of leaders fighting for change and equity across sectors. In addition, Danielle is a frequent speaker, active board member, and coach.

* * *

It was September 2020. We were six months into the pandemic in the United States. The unemployment rate had skyrocketed. Lines outside of food pantries circled long city blocks. Nonprofit workers were exhausted with no relief in sight for themselves or for the communities they were serving.

This quickly became the reality at East Boston Social Center (EBSC), a one hundred-year-old nonprofit in East Boston tucked between the runways of Logan Airport and the waters where the Charles River meets the Massachusetts Bay. Justin Pasqueriello, the organization's Executive Director, watched these widespread trends unfold within the four walls of the organization he had been running for three years. EBSC was staffed by frontline workers delivering childcare, education, nutrition, and elderly services in the historically low-income community of East Boston.

East Boston, where over 50 percent of residents are Latino, held the highest coronavirus positivity rate of the city at 15 percent of the population—an unwanted distinction held by neighborhoods across the country dominated by communities of color.

The EBSC staff were the workers who we were all reading about in headlines, saving lives and livelihoods in the heart of the pandemic. For Pasqueriello, they weren't headlines— they were his team members—and they were showing signs of exhaustion, burnout, and compassion fatigue.

Like most nonprofit leaders, Pasqueriello wasn't lacking the expertise and know-how to understand the challenge, but the resources to address it. Pasqueriello ultimately connected with a team of employees from Blue Cross Blue Shield of Massachusetts (BCBSMA) who helped him assess and address the issues of employee burnout. BCBSMA has a strong reputation in the Boston community for investing holistically in health outcomes, recognizing the environmental factors that contribute to overall health, and the value of mental health services. Together, they created an employee survey, an organizational culture statement, and a manager toolkit—immediate tools that allowed employees to know they were heard and gave managers the solutions to address employee burnout.

From afar, this seems like it would have been a very challenging time for a direct service nonprofit and a healthcare company to come together, figure out their complementary skills, and build smart mental health infrastructure. We were in a crisis. We were navigating one hour at a time. But these leaders and volunteers saw the need to address the big picture issues—and they found the space to prioritize it.

This story is an inspiring snapshot of the power of skills-based volunteering during a time of crisis—and this story is not unusual.

Doubling Down

The onset of the pandemic coincided with one of the most active moments of the year for volunteerism—National Volunteer Month in April. In late March, I remember thinking that we were inevitably going to see a complete shutdown of volunteer efforts, given the health concerns of direct volunteering and the massive disruption we were seeing in the workforce that was sure to impact virtual options.

While we did see a massive scale-down of in-person and hands-on volunteering with more than two thirds of volunteers being forced to stay home*, we saw a similarly dramatic rise in virtual and skills-based volunteering.† Individuals were even more intent to give their time and dollars as they saw the pandemic and resultant economic recession impact the livelihood of so many of their neighbors, and virtual skills-based volunteering became one of the few ways they felt they could do so safely. Many companies were eager to continue to serve their nonprofit partners and to engage the employees that had dispersed to their home offices across the country and globe.

After hearing dramatic stories for phoenix-from-the-ashes-like skilled volunteer efforts, I began to realize that my assumptions that volunteerism would entirely shutdown had underestimated the spirit of service that we hold so innately.

On April 1, I penned this note to Common Impact's community:

"It would be very easy in this time of uncertainty for our corporate partners to pull back from their service commitments—but instead, they're asking how they can be of additional support virtually from the safety of their employees' homes. It would be very easy for our nonprofit partners to turn down pro bono support as they fight new fires—but instead, they're reshaping their needs related to financial scenario

---

* Paul Sullivan, "Demands on Nonprofit Groups Rose During the Pandemic, Even as Volunteering Fell," New York Times, published November 20, 2020, https://www.nytimes.com/2020/11/13/your-money/nonprofit-groups-volunteers-pandemic.html.

† Mark Miller, "Virtual Volunteering Still Offers Benefits," New York Times, published October 28, 2020, https://www.nytimes.com/2020/10/28/business/retirement/seniors-volunteering.html.

planning, risk management, and crisis communication. It would be very easy for each of us in this moment of social distancing to pull back from one another, but what I've seen is the opposite."

And while the *ways* in which we volunteered—and the types of challenges that nonprofits called on for support—were fundamentally changed, the *desire, intent and connection* were still present and, in fact, amplified. This moment had opened our eyes to what was possible through virtual connection, and to the fact that skilled volunteering was accessible to individuals at all points in their career journey, and all nonprofits— from start-up to maturity, from crisis mode to stability.

Our team at Common Impact gained a greater understanding of how to shape skilled volunteering work to meet that wider variety of needs. We added hotline-type support for nonprofits in crisis, and broadscale training on topics such as business continuity and crisis communication.

In many ways, the best practices and tenets that the corporate volunteerism sector had built up over the years burst open and was suddenly much more accessible, flexible, and inclusive. With individuals across the globe suddenly able to engage in programs that were otherwise operating in regions far away, and with companies releasing grant restrictions, nonprofits were empowered to take the reins on getting the support they needed, thus expanding the reach and efficacy of skilled volunteering.

Bursting open at that same moment was a new era of racial awakening. The deep, systemic racism that we had tolerated and perpetuated for decades was coming under new scrutiny in an era of body cameras and social media. This awakening—and the resulting demand for advocacy and action—permeated across sectors. As businesses put out bold #BlackLivesMatter statements and commitments, they started looking to integrate those commitments into their skilled volunteering efforts.

As a white woman who is frustrated about the state of volunteering in our country, I am not proud to say that volunteering—as most of us know it—is white. Not the informal acts of kindness and service we see in our communities every day, but formal, structured volunteering. Donating your time and labor is a privileged activity, and often one that hasn't been as accessible to communities of color. And while companies have started to look at their employee and leadership diversity, most haven't fully begun to think about the deeply problematic racial lines of their volunteerism efforts. Teams of white professionals sweeping in to provide expertise to nonprofits that are often largely staffed by or serving communities of color reinforces the inequities and power dynamics that have plagued philanthropy since its inception.

It is here where those of us who are working toward social justice have started to see what has forever, not just momentarily, been changed by all that we experienced in 2020. We can no longer sweep contradictions under the proverbial rug. We cannot say #BlackLivesMatter without providing leadership and growth opportunities to Black employees. We can no longer say that we want to relieve the inequities experienced by communities of color without placing those communities in charge of the solutions they know we need.

In 2020, we started to understand that the social justice and social outcomes we were seeking weren't going to work with the barriers that we had erected to solve them. We learned about those barriers between philanthropists, volunteers, and we worked hard to overcome them. How?

Overcoming Obstacles

We gained respect for the capabilities largely resident in nonprofit and public sector employees that enabled us to respond to the pandemic swiftly and in force. We saw food banks lose a significant percentage of their workforce when volunteers needed to stay home but still meet the rapidly increasing demand as food insecurity rose. We saw domestic violence shelters and healthcare workers lean into the deepening mental health crisis that came along with the pandemic. We realized that what we often refer to offhandedly as "scrappy" nonprofit skills, are concrete, tangible talents that can benefit all sectors. We realized that those skills—of seeing the full landscape of need and rapidly reengineering operations to meet demand—were quite literally survival skills and would eat an MBA for breakfast.

In the corporate sector, we saw a loosening of the idea of roles. As employees stepped away from office buildings and city hubs, and employers started seeing the massive benefits of a virtual workforce, we stopped using company hierarchies and bureaucracies to determine what talents and roles workers could bring to volunteering. This had already started prepandemic with the "gig economy," but those same principles of identifying unique skill sets and targeting them toward particular business initiatives or challenges—for a moment in time, or as needed—started to permeate the corporate sector.

Today, we're seeing a much more sophisticated understanding across sectors of what talent means, how we can best leverage our people, and how we can provide the flexibility with roles and workplace culture that, theoretically, better enables them to bring their best.

So, what comes next? If we take advantage of this moment, we have the chance to break open what it means to build a career, to serve our communities, and to play a major role in tackling our world's largest challenges.

As these transformative forces—of the COVID-19 pandemic and the long overdue racial reckoning—move us away from shareholder capitalism to a more sustainable way of doing business and a more meaningful definition of personal success, we will see a more reciprocal, beneficial approach to service and volunteerism.

What do I mean? Shareholder capitalism created—or at least deepened—the divides between sectors, the privileged and the under resourced, the tradeoffs between personal and career success. As employees demand more from business than a paycheck, and as we continue to see the importance of amplifying the voices, perspectives, and skills of those traditionally overlooked, whether that be BIPOC leaders or stay-at-home parents, we'll move away from a service sector focused on giving and volunteerism flowing in one direction toward a reciprocal flow of the rich community, business, and personal perspectives that, together, pave the quickest path to the solution.

At Common Impact, we refer to this as The Knitting Factor™. The Knitting Factor represents the ultimate potential of skills-based volunteerism. There are three components to The Knitting Factor that we saw—in the partnership between EBSC and BCBSM—and that we see in the future of skills-based volunteering:

- **Panoramic perspective:** A view that looks at people beyond their titles, organizations, and sectors to allow value to transcend profit.
- **Skill sharing:** A focus on two-way talent exchange, where skilled volunteers learn as much from the nonprofit leaders they work with as those leaders learn from them.
- **Sticky relationships:** A commitment to building long lasting partnerships that drive missions and business forward.

When done well, skills-based volunteerism enables the exchange and knitting together of skills from the business and nonprofit community—not a transactional donation of them. It heavily values the community and cultural competencies that allow smart "on paper" organizational strategies to have their intended outcomes. It facilitates the cocreation, coownership, and coaccountability for social outcomes.

This is not just the future of skilled volunteering. This is the future of community and employee engagement.

"Never let a good crisis go to waste." Leaders as diverse as Winston Churchill and Rahm Emannuel understood that there is an opportunity in crisis moments. It teaches us that our behavior can change, quickly and fundamentally, when the stakes are high enough. And, as we look at the realities, such as climate change and the structural inequities that continue to plague life as we know it, the stakes couldn't be higher.

Right now—today—is the moment to take what we learned from the interlocking crises of 2020, and usher in a new generation of skills-based, equity-driven volunteerism.

The Power of Informal Volunteerism

Karmit Bulman is the Executive Director of the Minnesota Alliance for Volunteer Advancement (MAVA). MAVA supplies cutting edge volunteer engagement resources that enable organizations and individuals to meet critical community needs. Karmit oversees strategic planning, board development, financial management, fundraising, program development, and day-to-day programming at MAVA. Karmit has authored multiple articles and research reports on strategic volunteer engagement, including work on job equity for volunteer engagement professionals, race equity, tapping into the strengths of older volunteers, and connecting formal and informal volunteers. Karmit helped found The National Alliance for Volunteer Engagement and serves on the leadership team and cochairs the engaging funder workgroup. Prior to her role at MAVA, Karmit was the executive director for the Conflict Resolution Center, Temple Israel, Vail Place, and Avenues for Homeless Youth. Karmit firmly believes that increased volunteer infrastructure can improve lives and communities.

* * *

I am the Executive Director of the Minnesota Alliance for Volunteer Advancement (MAVA). I am also a Jewish woman, activist, and volunteer. I grew up with an imperative to "repair the world." I live in the Twin Cities, close to where George Floyd was murdered and just blocks from neighborhoods destroyed in the aftermath of his murder. MAVA has been focused on formal volunteerism and diversity, equity, and inclusion in volunteerism for many years. But it wasn't until the events of 2020 that my perspective truly shifted. Here is why.

Emerging from the COVID Cocoon

It is spring 2020. We are on edge following Floyd's murder. We have been ordered to stay at home. COVID-related deaths and severe illnesses keep us on high alert, and we are in a constant state of uncertainty and fear. What motivated thousands of us to flock to what is now known as "George Floyd Square" with our shovels, garbage bags, and hygiene supplies to clean up neighborhoods torn apart by civil unrest? No one organized us. No formal organization called upon us to do community clean-up. What motivated us to leave our COVID cocoons? How did we manage success with no one there to organize us—no organization to check our backgrounds, orient us, or provide us with a job description and a supervisor?

For me, the past two years have been a glaring wake-up call about the power of informal volunteerism. As a professional in the field and a lifelong formal and informal volunteer, it is time for me to more carefully be the advocate I want for my community, state, and nation through more appropriate engagement of both formal and informal volunteers.

During this horrific time, I am flabbergasted by the knee-jerk response of most organizations who furlough volunteers and lay off volunteer engagement professionals. As director of an organization dedicated to promoting and supporting volunteerism, I receive call after call from my professional volunteer leader friends who have been let go. I am also worried about my volunteer friends, once so very essential to the places where they volunteered but now deemed a liability. I wonder how we will take care of vulnerable community members without the tireless efforts of frontline organized volunteers.

I search online and I learn that in every corner of the world, people are responding to the serious problems caused by COVID-19 through what our profession calls "informal volunteering." In fact, 70 percent of the world's volunteers are informal.*

Personal Sense of Responsibility

The drive to help others during a crisis comes from a basic desire to exercise a very personal sense of responsibility to our neighbors and our communities. People may prefer to respond in their own way and on their own time to address what they feel is wrong. Even as formal volunteering arose during the twentieth century, informal volunteering has been the prevalent form of service for centuries. Also, as Ms. Vang-Roberts

---

* According to the United Nations's "State of the World's Volunteerism Report 2018: The Thread that Binds," 70 percent of the world's volunteerism is conducted informally.

discussed in her chapter about racial equity in volunteerism, informal volunteerism is a way of life for many communities of color and immigrant communities who participate, contribute, serve, and help others in their daily lives but don't refer to those acts of service as volunteering.

COVID-19 and the resulting restrictions offer us an opportunity to rethink our old norms. Many organizations had to shut down or curtail formal volunteering, yet in many respects volunteerism was more alive than ever. People knew the dangers of COVID-19, however, many were still willing to assume the risks. They knew that their service was needed more than ever during a pandemic.

In addition, George Floyd's and other racially unjust murders, combined with pandemic-related health disparities, activated a strong surge of race equity action. During the pandemic, it has become clear that our formal approaches to volunteer engagement may unintentionally create barriers for many people who wish to volunteer. We have set up systems and processes for engaging volunteers: a volunteer application, formal screening and interviewing of candidates, a comprehensive orientation, background checks, job descriptions, a volunteer handbook, and a clearly communicated chain of command. These are all best practices, right? We may learn the answer to that question by again recognizing that 70 percent of the world's population volunteer outside of an organizational structure.

People flock toward informal volunteering because they can reach people in ways that organizations cannot. Where there are systems, procedures, and processes, people can fall through the cracks. In informal volunteering, people see that others need support and they can jump right in. When we have connections with neighbors or community members, we reach out to assist. We may not even call this volunteering. The support provided is more personal and directly connected to the needs of a community.

This Change is Everything

My own experience as an informal volunteer is a case in point. The impact of the pandemic motivated me to connect with an elderly widower who had been devastated by isolation and grief during this period of stay-at-home orders and fear of life-threatening illness. A few of us have become the volunteer family to our elder friend. Our phone calls, walks, visits, food drop-offs, birthday and holiday celebrations, and home maintenance projects are lifesavers to our friend. Our interaction is not restricted by barriers often set up by risk management concerns of formal organizations. We take care of our friend because of the connection we have formed with him.

I have reached out to many other informal volunteers, many of them people of color. Their stories demonstrate the impact of informal volunteerism. Many have participated in formal volunteering, but when they reflect on the activities where they have had the most impact, it is clear that informal volunteering tends to be overlooked and undervalued.

Christian McCleary is a twenty-five-year-old volunteer who works informally to help Black men succeed. He recently ran for public office and has served as an AmeriCorps VISTA, where he prioritized advocating for the Black community in admittedly very formal volunteer roles. But Christian also hosts a podcast and he regularly speaks out about community building, equity, and politics. When Christian was seventeen, he withdrew from high school and got involved politically by discussing police and community relations in Washington, D.C., and meeting White House officials. For Christian, waiting for an organization to accept him as a volunteer on *their* terms was unnecessary. With so much work to do around racial equality, Christian just rolls up his sleeves and gets it done. He has chosen the informal. He doesn't wait for an invitation. He speaks up and takes action.

Jewelean Jackson is another community gem. She is a seventy-two-year-old board chair for the University of Minnesota Community University Health Center. She advocates on behalf of those with a history of medical injustices and lack of healthcare access. Jewelean holds the title for Lifetime National Ms. Kwanzaa. Her embrace of the Kwanzaa way of life—unity, self-determination, collective work and responsibility, cooperative economics, purpose, creativity, and earth—drive her informal volunteer leadership as founder of Twin Cities Juneteenth, which has led to more formal volunteer roles including founding the Children's Defense Fund Minnesota Freedom Schools and Miss Black Minnesota Pageant Inc.

Then there is Jaylen Lens, who recently became a formal volunteer coordinator at a Minneapolis nonprofit. Jaylen's grandfather told him, "We take care of our community," and Jaylen has informally volunteered his whole life. He just never called it volunteering. Taking care of sick relatives and neighbors, watching young kids, and protesting injustice—these actions are woven into the fabric of Jaylen's family. As a professional volunteer coordinator today, Jaylen is working to relax formal volunteering barriers in organizations that engage volunteers so that BIPOC can more easily formally volunteer for campaigns to end homelessness, reduce the achievement gap, and enhance career readiness. Jaylen is crucial to uniting the informal and the formal.

It is important to prioritize listening to informal volunteers. At MAVA, we host listening sessions for informal BIPOC volunteers. They have told us to create different ways of volunteering, which may include different pathways for different people, removing barriers, and/or compensating volunteers. Their words were loud and clear: We need to prioritize BIPOC leadership at organizations engaging volunteers. It is up to us to build trust between nonprofit organizations and BIPOC communities. It is time to foster a welcoming environment and culture within formal organizations and within volunteer structures. Our listening sessions reminded us of the need to value people over organization and put the community's needs first. It is time to understand systemic barriers and to tear down and rebuild when necessary.

The pandemic has offered opportunities to learn from and reach out to informal volunteers who are caring for those in need. Informal volunteers may do their own work, or they may form or join informal volunteer groups. A visit to George Floyd Square is a good example. People have set up tables to distribute clothes, food, and hygiene supplies they have personally collected. Individuals stand in the square and initiate conversations encouraging others to take action to address race-related police violence.

Mutual aid groups are emerging everywhere. Groups like

Minnesota COVID Sitters,* St. Louis Quarantine Support,†
Students Against Corona,‡ and 9+6 Seattle§ demonstrate that
people looking to help during a pandemic are not always
inclined to volunteer formally at an organization. People
want to help, and we need to remove the barriers that have
prevented them from volunteering formally. Our standard
definitions and measures of what constitutes volunteer activity do not adequately account for the freely given time and
effort which, in a more inclusive framework of understanding,
would be regarded as volunteering. Volunteer activity is no less
important and no less an economic and social contribution,
whether taking place within a formal organizational setting or
an informal community context.

The acts often associated with informal volunteering (visiting an elderly neighbor, giving advice, looking after a prop-
erty, or looking after a friend's pet) are more likely to happen
without realizing that the activity registers as volunteering.
Fortunately, technology has made informal volunteerism
even more convenient for many. We can reach out to isolated
community members by Facetime or video chat. We can order
food and supplies online and arrange for delivery to those in
need without leaving our own homes.

Less rigid definitions of volunteerism are needed to fully
recognize and value contributions of all kinds. Particular attention should be given to the cultural and legal liability that are

---

* MN Covid Sitters, https://www.mncovidsitters.org/.
† St. Louis Quarantine Support, https://www.facebook.com/STLQuarantine-Support/.
‡ Students Against Corona, http://studentsagainstcorona.co.uk/.
§ Covid19 Mutual Aid—Seattle, https://www.facebook.com/covid19mutu-alaid/.

often identified as key barriers to organizational outreach to informal volunteers. More adaptive and inclusive models of volunteerism are needed to harness the capacities and resilience that exist within and across communities. Our current practices and structure may be counterproductive. Given the increasing needs caused by the pandemic and other challenges (climate change and racial injustice, for example), it is likely that informal volunteers will provide much of the additional surge capacity required to respond to more frequent emergencies and disasters in the future.

While informal volunteering plays a vital role in communities, it is important to acknowledge that it will never replace formal volunteerism. For example, when thousands of us showed up at George Floyd Square with our shovels, garbage bags, and hygiene supplies, my first thought was: "Where are the volunteer engagement professionals?" We needed the coordination and structure that formal volunteerism offers. Informal volunteerism will never meet all community needs and tends to lack strategy and prioritization. There are many areas of community needs where volunteerism is essential, yet these efforts cannot be replaced by informal volunteering. For example, disaster relief, massive food distribution, and ecosystem restoration require a tremendous amount of strategy, intentionality, and structure. There are community efforts that require subject matter expertise and a solid understanding of the complex systems at play to effectively address the issue or problem. For example, community mediation and mental health volunteers need training, expertise, and the formality associated with organizational volunteerism.

With 70 percent of volunteerism in the world done informally, now is the time for volunteer engagement leaders to connect with those informal volunteers. There is a reason why most people choose informal over formal volunteering. Get curious and see what informal volunteers can teach us. Improvisation and innovation are key features of informal volunteerism. Consider reaching out to organized informal groups (such as mutual aid societies) and loosely connected informal groups (such as those handing out masks and hand-sanitizers in under-resourced areas).

Let's ask ourselves the question, "How can we change our volunteer engagement practices and expand the definition of best practices to be more inclusive and less rigid?" On the flip side, can we offer to collaborate and share some of our organizational resources with informal volunteers? Perhaps some of the tips and tools used by professionals would be useful to those engaged informally? Now is the time to connect the informal with the formal for better impact for all.

Volunteering as a Mechanism to Develop Empathy

Chris Jarvis and Angela Parker

Chris Jarvis's (he/him) research and presentations focus on corporate citizenship as a powerful mechanism to address the critical social and environmental issues facing our global society. Chris has over twenty-five years of experience working with corporate and nonprofit executives to develop results-based impact strategies. He is a renowned public speaker and author with education and experience in the fields of neuroscience, organizational change, behavioral insights, and transformative learning. In 2015, Chris cofounded Realized Worth Institute (RWI), a think tank focused on advancing the practice and theory of corporate volunteering through innovative projects, research, analysis, and public policy change. As the cofounder, Chris is the company's Chief Strategy Officer and provides guidance as a Senior Advisor to the company's Client Delivery team.

Angela Parker's (she/her) work focuses on the practical application of transformative learning theory in corporate settings. Her background is in communications, entrepreneurship, and strategy execution. She has consulted with over one hundred large companies globally, started and sold small businesses, worked within nonprofit organizations, and provided workshops and training all over the world. Angela has been published in various books and magazines such as *CSR for HR* by Elaine Cohen, *Cause Marketing for Dummies* by Joe Waters, *Volunteer Engagement 2.0* by Rob Rosenthal, and others. Angela earned her master of business administration from IE Business School in Madrid, Spain, and recently completed a three-year appointment as President of the Board for Renewal in the Wilderness. As the cofounder of the Realized Worth Institute (RWI), Angela is the company's CEO and provides guidance as a Senior Advisor to the company's Client Delivery team concepts and more.

* * *

Several years ago, I taught a class at New York University of Abu Dhabi on Corporate Volunteering. The session was optional, but the room was packed with students. They were highly engaged, and the discussion was lively, but there was one young woman in the room who sat slumped and scowling throughout the entire presentation. By the end of the session, I could hardly wait to speak with her.

When I asked her opinion of the session, she looked at me for a long second before flatly stating, "I think corporate volunteering is bullshit."

I almost hugged her. What is more interesting than a student who actually has a viewpoint? She agreed to sit down and tell me her story:

"I worked for [a large utilities company based in the US] last summer. They hold this huge fundraising run every year and they give employees time off to either run in the event or support it during the day. I'm not a runner, but I like being outside and social causes are really important to me. I signed up and got the information and when I showed up, it had a cool vibe. People were running around, getting things set up, and I was given an assignment pretty quickly.

"After I finished my first task, I started looking around for people from work so I could find out what to do next. When I finally found someone, she told me I could hang out at the water table until the runners started coming through and then she said, 'But it doesn't really matter. Just enjoy the day off work.' I didn't think much about that at the time, but later I went back to one of the busses to get more water bottles and found a bunch of people from work just chilling there. I don't know why I bothered, but I decided to ask, 'Why are you here if you're not volunteering?' One woman—and I know she's a manager—said, 'My job sucks, honey. I deserve the time off.'

"Corporate Volunteering Is Bullshit"

"I went back to the water table after that, but honestly, I just felt shitty. I know I never want her to be my manager. And I know no one really cares about this. And basically, corporate volunteering is bullshit."

This young woman's story is a worst-case scenario. Most managers are not likely to blatantly misrepresent their companies at a volunteer event, but even with the disappointing manager in the picture, that fundraising event could have been a deeply meaningful experience for participants. It could have been an experience that motivated the young woman to become an advocate for volunteering and social impact.

Instead, it did the opposite.

2020, the Catalyst

Now, more than ever, volunteering has the potential to fill an important gap. The global pandemic and the widely viewed murder of George Floyd in 2020 shook loose a deep and latent need for change within human beings. It extended even to the level of organizations and corporations as people who had been categorized as "colleague" or "manager" shared each other's grief and began to experience a new and unexpected sense of shared humanity.

In the wake of 2020, an unprecedented number of companies came to Realized Worth Institute (RWI) asking not only to build employee volunteer programs, but also to leverage them to cultivate more of these humanizing encounters. Not every company knew exactly what they were asking for, but they had seen that deep and latent need reveal itself in the unrest around them. It was not a need to give back. It was not a need to make a difference. It was not even a need to help. It was a need for *empathy*.

Collective empathy was the greatest outgrowth of 2020. George Floyd's primal cries for his mother were all of our cries. His head under the knee of the oppressor was each of our heads. People didn't pause, analyze, and logically conclude, "Empathy is what we need!"—people rose up in protest. They rioted. They said, "No more!" As they cried out for the honor of the man who was killed, they fought for the remnants of humanity left in their own hearts. People don't have to decide we need empathy to develop empathy. We just need encounters where we can no longer avoid seeing ourselves in the other.

When it comes to volunteering, it became clear that painting walls and planting trees was not enough. It became embarrassing. In 2020, corporate executives said, "Build me a volunteering program that changes the hearts and minds of the people that run this company." They began to understand that policy change and new laws will help, but they will not heal the virus that feeds racism, homophobia, sexism, and violence. Only empathy will. Only the physiological change that takes place in our brains when we intentionally challenge the assumptions that got us here. Only the eradication of "us versus them."

Volunteering plays a key role in developing empathy when it is intentionally built as an arena within which to invite people, in safe and nonthreatening ways, to face and grapple with their complicity. The opportunity and responsibility of companies to build social impact programs with this intention is perhaps our greatest hope. The influence of the corporation on the lives of individuals—their finances, their mental health, their families, the way they vote—is society-shaping. If companies continue to offer volunteering solely for the sake of volunteering, we will see systemic oppression persist. The same systemic oppression that led to the murder of George Floyd. Changing hearts and minds is no small task, but we do not have time for anything less.

What Do People Want from Volunteering?

In the wake of 2020, RWI's clients are newly aware that volunteering for the sake of volunteering is not enough. It does not meet the deeply felt needs of society. It does not meet the needs of the protestor, the rioter, the ones crying for justice. It is not what we want.

In general, we know what we want in life. We want stability and motivation. We want adventure and meaning. We want to love and be loved. When we aren't experiencing these things, we diagnose ourselves and we search for a solution. When we *are* experiencing these things, we tell stories about solutions that surprised us. We can't always trust our ability to accurately diagnose ourselves or to prescribe the right solution, but we *can* trust our ability to recognize the solution when it finds us. When we have what we want, we say, "This is it! This is what I've been looking for!"

"This is it! This is what I've been looking for!" is what people want to get out of a volunteer experience. It is not, however, what they say they want. Try asking yourself, "What do you want to get out of a volunteer experience?" You might say, "I want it to be meaningful and aligned with my personal passions. I want it to be fun. I want to connect with others. I want to learn something." These are true for most people. In fact, most volunteer experiences are designed with these outcomes in mind. In response to employee surveys, companies typically choose cause areas based on what employees care about; volunteer events are organized and set up with food, music, and social elements. There are often opportunities for learning, using skills, and connecting with others. So, why does it remain so difficult to motivate people to volunteer?

"Meaningful," "fun," and "passion-aligned" are elements that can be referred to as hygiene factors. Hygiene factors, in life or work, do not generate positive satisfaction or motivation. They are, rather, the basic elements that bring the score to "neutral" on a rating scale of dissatisfied to satisfied. To get beyond neutral, "motivators" are required. Motivators arise from the intrinsic conditions of the experience, such as interesting driving social movements, interacting with individuals affected by oppression, and challenging our biases and assumptions. If volunteer experiences are missing the basic hygiene factors, they will almost always fail. (This rule typically does not apply when it comes to natural disasters or other highly intense or unusual volunteer experiences. Motivators are built into these experiences due to their heightened circumstances.) If the basic hygiene factors are *not* missing, the volunteer experience will be fine. It might even be fun. But it won't be what volunteers want—not really. In many cases, the lack of motivators will leave volunteers uninterested in participating again.

"This Is It! This Is What I Want!"

Social activists and community advocates are born out of volunteer experiences that leave participants with clear answers to three questions:

1. Can you imagine the lives of the people the volunteer experience is meant to benefit (the beneficiary)?
2. What story will you tell others about this experience after it's over?

3. What connects this volunteer experience to our group and its purpose?

Imagining the lives of the beneficiary is about challenging assumptions. For too long, volunteering has been about "making a difference" for others. Powerful and well-resourced groups drop in to help communities become more like them. This is an objectifying posture. It is a posture that separates "us" from "them." The less we consider that "the other" may in fact be just like us, the less likely we are to develop empathy and *act on behalf* of our shared human experience. On the other hand, the more we make conscious decisions to put ourselves in situations where our assumptions are challenged, the more likely we are to recognize our sameness and act accordingly. Volunteering, however, rarely challenges our assumptions—especially not when it fails to go beyond hygiene factors to integrate motivators.

Create the Conditions

Give volunteers what they want—empower them to participate in deconstructing systems of oppression—by making volunteering an arena within which to face and wrestle with implicit biases. At the beginning of every volunteer experience, invite participants to imagine the lives of the beneficiary. Tell them, "The poor are not a problem to be solved. The poor are not 'the poor.' The men and women we will serve today are told every day, 'Get off my stoop. Go get a job. Get out of my way.'

"The most important thing we will do today is say, 'You are worth my time.' So, sit down with them. Listen to their stories. Tell yours. Allow yourself to be affected." Challenge the assumptions of participants who have not yet considered that the beneficiary may have as much to offer as they do. Alert the minds of participants to new and unexpected possibilities.

If the beneficiary cannot be in proximity to volunteers, create proximity with a different kind of invitation. Tell them, "Today we'll organize this supplies room so that single mothers who live in this community can choose what they need and provide for their families. Take a minute to think about one of the mothers who will come here. Her name might be...Sarah. She might be working two jobs and have her three young kids in daycare. She's smart and she's strong and she's tired. Every night when she gets home with her kids, it takes everything she's got to make them dinner and spend time together before falling asleep and starting again the next day. Imagine Sarah. Imagine her house and what she looks like. Imagine her kids. Now, take a minute to share with the person next to you: If you're Sarah, what's your greatest fear?"

This invitation at the beginning of volunteer experiences will look and sound different in different scenarios, but the intended outcome is always a clear answer to the question, "Can you imagine the lives of the people the volunteer experience is meant to benefit (the beneficiary)?" Use this as a litmus test. An invitation that also challenges assumptions (e.g., "The poor are not a problem to be solved.") is what will lead to a clear answer to the next question, "What story will you tell others about this experience after it's over?"

When human beings are presented with new and surprising information, our first instinct is to use it to increase social capital. We like the way we feel when we are excited by new ideas, and we want to be the source of that feeling for someone else. Engagement is sharing. Sharing stories about an experience is the best way to measure an individual's level of engagement. Participants will have a compelling story to tell if the invitation to imagine the beneficiary includes a challenge to their assumptions.

Making the Connection

To reiterate an important point, "This is it! This is what I've been looking for!" is what people want to get out of a volunteer experience. Here's how:

- Creating conditions for that feeling to occur requires proximity to the beneficiary (even if we must paint a mental picture to create a sense of proximity) and a challenge to the assumptions participants arrived with, which results in a compelling story to share.
- For it to matter that your group is doing this together, employees must be empowered to achieve greater impact by volunteering *with* your group or organization than they could achieve by volunteering on their own. Without a direct connection back to your group (Why are we doing this as a group? How does it connect to us and our purpose?), participants may have a transformative volunteering experience, but the outcomes of that experience will not benefit the organization or the individuals as it relates to the purpose of the organization.

- Every group volunteer experience must provide a clear answer to the question, "What connects this volunteer experience to our group and its purpose?" This connection enables participants to develop affective commitment. In contrast to normative commitment and continuance commitment, affective commitment is an emotional attachment to the organization that motivates productivity and long-term retention.

When the basic hygiene factors are in place, the added elements that illustrate the answers to the three questions are what become motivators. The key, however, is creating conditions in which participants arrive at the answers *when they're ready*.

Not every volunteer is open to being moved, challenged, or even surprised by volunteering. For those volunteers, the hygiene factors are enough.

But when they're ready, and when the conditions are available, volunteers will respond with deep and surprising satisfaction, gradually finding their way to becoming effective activists and advocates who invite others into the same experience.

This is when they'll hear their inner voice telling them, "This is it! This is what I've been looking for!"

Rethinking Engagement

Service Days: Changing the Conversation

Beth Steinhorn and Jerome Tennille

Beth Steinhorn: As president of VQ Volunteer Strategies, Beth partners with organizations and their leadership to increase impact through strategic and innovative volunteer engagement.

Jerome Tennille is a Corporate Responsibility and Social Impact strategist who works in the hospitality industry and advises on volunteerism independently.

* * *

As engagement professionals, we are accustomed to encountering the "Days of Service" conundrum—Jerome Tennille from the corporate perspective as a manager leading corporate social responsibilities initiatives and volunteer opportunities for a hospitality company and Beth Steinhorn from the perspective as a volunteer engagement consultant to nonprofit leaders. This is our recent conversation about Days of Service and the emerging opportunities to change the paradigm for the better, along with our ideas to encourage others to engage in similar discussions.

The Challenge

Beth Steinhorn (BS): Days of service have been formalized for decades, whether associated with a heritage month, a religious or secular holiday such as Veterans Day, or the well-known, federally recognized days such as Martin Luther King Jr. Day and September 11 as National Day of Service and Remembrance. Despite their popularity, days of service are a double-edged sword.

On the positive side, they are an effective device to raise the profile of volunteering in our communities, garnering great media attention. With volunteers increasingly seeking short-term or flexible volunteer opportunities, a day of service is a way to reach new volunteers. And, for those organizations with meaningful projects that require large numbers of people to accomplish them—like building a playground or planting trees—a day of service can effectively attract the workforce needed to get the work done quickly. But let's be honest—such meaningful large-scale projects are generally the exception rather than the rule, which leads us to the other side of this double-edged sword.

Days of service are often a burden to nonprofit leaders. Finding—or worse yet, *creating*—projects for large groups of volunteers to do in one day has long been a challenge. As a consultant and trainer, I am regularly asked by nonprofit professionals how to "handle" the requests by corporate partners to provide opportunities for—and this is but an example: "Thirty-eight people in matching t-shirts to do something meaningful in three hours."

Volunteer directors often feel caught between expectations by fund development goals and mission-driven program needs. As such, they occasionally resort to prioritizing the corporate or service group request by creating work that doesn't necessarily serve the needs of the program.

You have worked on both the nonprofit and corporate side, Jerome. How have you navigated these challenges?

Jerome Tennille (JT): To more fully support the creation, design, planning, and implementation of Corporate Social Responsibility (CSR) programs, I lean on my experience managing volunteer programs in the nonprofit sector. While a different sector and mission, much of the work in CSR is identical; the difference is the lens that I apply when shaping corporate employee volunteer programs. So, it's not lost on me as a practitioner the additional requirements that may be placed on a nonprofit when they host a day of service during a period like the holidays or on a day that bears historical significance like MLK Day of Service.

Some even suggest that the single day of service—particularly those celebrated on the same day annually—is just a symbolic gesture. Yet, the gesture can come at great expense for the nonprofit organizations that host these events. Also, in many instances—especially here in the United States—we sometimes forget it may be a national holiday or recognized day off. That's most certainly the case when volunteering on

MLK Jr. Day of Service. But for many nonprofits—particularly those that are understaffed and overworked—there's pressure to meet society's collective desire to serve. This sometimes creates great pressure to meet that societal demand, even if at their own peril.

In my work, I try very hard to listen to the voice of the community. Here's an example: In January 2020, I suggested a different approach to MLK Jr. Day of Service. I had three objectives. First, I wanted to use this nationally recognized day of service to launch additional volunteering tools. Secondly, I wanted to rethink the paradigm of the single day of service by encouraging year-round volunteering. Lastly, we had to be sensitive to employees' time constraints as we wrapped up a string of campaigns through November and December. So, in lieu of a volunteer project on MLK Day of Service, we sent through an educational communique with the tools to empower and equip, while reinforcing the message to consider volunteering throughout the remainder of the year. Here's why: That particular day is, in fact, a day off, so the corporate-sponsored volunteer activity would have to take place the preceding Friday. But, more importantly, I wanted to be sensitive to the possibility that by supporting MLK Jr. Day of Service through erecting a group volunteer project, there may be unintentional consequences—namely, unwittingly promoting behaviors that reinforce the idea of one-and-done volunteering.

Additionally, it's easy to observe that these designated days of service garner a lot of attention, often from large groups. In my experience, such activities may communicate a falsity that having more volunteers equates to achieving better outcomes, when that's not how all critical issues are solved across the globe. When you peel the onion further, the traditional day of service may even reinforce other issues of privilege, savior complex, or what I describe as an uneven power balance between large entities and their smaller nonprofit partners. In many cases, when all is said and done, volunteering on MLK Jr. Day of Service becomes just a nice gesture, a symbolic act that may not necessarily do right by the community.

Being aware of these potential shortcomings helped us chart a more expansive strategy: We launched a successful communications campaign focused on encouraging year-round volunteer service, education about critical issues, and how to champion volunteerism with a new toolkit designed to empower and equip employees to serve based on the current needs of the community. The idea was akin to teaching a village how to fish, not just giving them the fish. What I didn't realize at the time is that the landscape of service would forever change in a way that supported this idea just weeks later as the COVID-19 outbreak reached the United States. The tragic events associated with the pandemic forced people to look with fresh eyes at the idea that service shouldn't be limited to just a specific day, nor should it be forced or coupled with a time of year that may run counter to the needs of an organization.

From your experience as a consultant, Beth, what patterns did you observe as nonprofits navigated days of service amid the pandemic restrictions?

Transformations and Recommendations

BS: By summer of 2020, as community needs changed and increased due to the economic despair resulting from the pandemic, days of service were reimagined by many organizations and completely dismantled by others. As income inequality and poverty increased, so did food insecurity, inspiring many nonprofit and CSR professionals to focus on buoying up the social safety net which requires more than a one-time engagement.

Prior to 2020, serving meals or packing food at a food distribution center, soup kitchen, or residential organization was the go-to volunteer activity for families, employees, students, and other groups. Historically in the weeks prior to a day of service, groups would hastily contact a nonprofit organization and express their desire to volunteer, also sharing the group's narrow parameters (e.g., accommodating a group of at least a dozen people, often with a photo opportunity built in). In many instances, this meant a one-time activity. Yet, hunger is a complex issue which will never be solved by simply providing a few meals.

But 2020 was different from prior years in that many people who had never previously needed it sought food and financial assistance. While, sadly, food insecurity was nothing new, the pandemic and resulting economic downturn dramatically and suddenly increased the needs for social services and for year-round volunteer support, not just a single day. Meanwhile, many employees, now working remotely due to stay-at-home orders, had more flexibility. Some food pantries and senior service organizations, for example, successfully connected with companies to engage employees on a monthly or weekly basis to make wellness calls to isolated seniors, sort and pack food in pantries, or run errands on behalf of neighbors.

Through these partnerships, many organizations relegated days of service to a relic of the past, giving life, instead, to new, ongoing opportunities, untethered to a significant date in history.

Jerome, let's get back to what you were talking about earlier. You were describing how you'd planted the seeds of change in your organization before the arrival of the pandemic. How did these changes actually play out after the COVID-19 outbreak?

JT: Unsurprisingly, we did not host a volunteer activity in January 2021. Of course, this was very much connected to the ongoing pandemic and the necessity to keep safe, healthy, and reduce the risk of contracting the virus, as most Americans were not yet vaccinated. But, upon reflection, the pandemic was a catalyst that gave everyone permission to think creatively about how we would engage in service moving forward. The pandemic, though catastrophic, brought about important changes to the nonprofit, government, and private sectors that have helped us expand beyond the age-old practices to which we were bound. These changes have, in many ways, helped to break the chains that bound us to age-old practices that may not be a necessary tactic to solving the issues we face socially and environmentally.

I believe these changes are long overdue. Despite their good intentions, days of service can deepen cracks of inequity in our society by reinforcing misconceptions and presenting quick solutions to complex, systemic challenges. While giving back to others is obviously a good thing, it can unintentionally cause harm to others, silently undermine the very issues we're seeking to solve, perpetuate injustices, and force cultural norms onto others.

Here, I'd like to share a few recommendations to help the sector leverage the innovations from our pandemic era days of service to fuel an evolved vision for days of service.

- In the same way that I chose to introduce a new way to acknowledge MLK Day of Service, embracing an educational communique and supplemental toolkit to inspire year-round volunteering, we should collectively work toward a message of "commit to serve." Simply put, we must work to inspire individuals to sign up and serve in the future weeks or months when needs are still pressing. In thinking back to MLK Day of Service, what most in society don't immediately realize is that nonprofits often experience an overwhelming surge of support in January, followed by a sharp downturn shortly thereafter, leaving many volunteer-involving organizations in a drought in the months of February, March, April, and May. *This must change.*

- Secondly, we must also consider the power of evolving the day of service to become equally understood as a day of reflection and learning. I believe learning is an action. If we understand learning through that lens, then perhaps lending our time to simply being educated by nonprofits solving critical issues—namely the subject matter experts—can be a form of service. A volunteer who learns and reflects is the same volunteer who will walk away a better citizen, more fully informed on the issues affecting his or her community. If we really want to get beyond vanity volunteering and engage people to address root causes of hunger and poverty, for example, we must incorporate learning into these days so that we tap into the best of effective service learning, which includes learning, service, and reflection.

Beth, what recommendations do you have to add?

BS: We must equip leaders of volunteers and organizations to confidently have the difficult conversations with companies and businesses, faith-based organizations, community, and groups that approach with the offer to bring that group of t-shirt clad volunteers eager to "do something meaningful." We must get to the roots of understanding whose needs are really being met through the day of service. We also must do more to create the tools and resources necessary that allow these social impact and volunteer engagement professionals to explain the challenges that large group projects may pose, sharing impactful alternatives that may look different, and even saying no, and doing all of this with comfort, courage, and confidence. Similarly, we must empower leaders of volunteers to have these discussions with organizational executives and board members and with funders.

- Finally, we should continue the effort to evolve the ways we track and measure impact and communicate success. If we continue to focus on the *number* of volunteers and the hours served as the primary measure of success, then we will inevitably sustain the "more is better" myth. However, if we focus instead on outputs and outcomes—including the support and comfort delivered by volunteers who check in with isolated adults, the skills pro bono employees can help develop by mentoring nonprofit professionals, and the resilience that communities experience from a stronger network of neighbors—then we will see the value of shifting from single days of service to new paradigms that serve our communities better.

Technology and Services Are Poised to Create WIDER Nonprofits

Doug Bolton

Doug Bolton is a trained journalist with experience in print, broadcast, digital, and all forms of media. He spent thirty years in the media business, including nearly fifteen years as a business journal publisher. In 2011, he was recruited to run a geographic division of what is now the world's second largest commercial real estate services firm. Community nonprofit leadership roles led Doug to begin working in 2018 with Inspiring Service founders Craig and Michael Young on deploying technology and services to more efficiently and effectively build volunteer ecosystem infrastructure for hands-on service to board-level leadership.

***

Most of the world had never heard George Floyd's name nor were we aware of a devastating coronavirus called

COVID-19 when the nonprofit Inspiring Service was awarded the highest innovation award by the Independent Sector for its board-matching platform.

The recognition in November 2019 by the Independent Sector, the nation's most eclectic membership organization committed to creating a civil society, validated what Inspiring Service had been hearing and seeing from users of its technology and community leaders since its 2017 inception.

Focus on WIDER Nonprofit Boards Shifted

In creating infrastructure to help prospective volunteers find active nonprofits in ways the nonprofit sector has never experienced, Inspiring Service long recognized that the traditional ways of recruiting nonprofit board members were failing in creating "WIDER"—welcoming, inclusive, diverse, equitable, and representative—nonprofit boards. The largely homogeneous makeup of our nation's nonprofit boards was contributing to the pervasive, ongoing problems in our society, from poverty to hunger to the deepening mental health care crisis.

With support from its primary funder and the promises of funding from other communities excited by the board matching innovation, Inspiring Service planned to rapidly expand its board platform in 2020 with the intent of driving millions of dollars in impact for the nation.

Then the pandemic hit.

Enlightened community leaders across the country who had begun thinking about implementing Inspiring Service's board matching platform suddenly found themselves faced with catastrophic challenges for the nonprofits and communities they supported. What they quickly realized was that the economics of WIDER nonprofit boards are considerable: As hard as finding diverse candidates is for most nonprofit boards, their value would likely be considerably greater than an average board member.

While Independent Sector calculates the value of a volunteer hour ($28.54) and Common Impact, a twenty-year-old nonprofit helping companies and nonprofits engage better together, calculates the value of a skilled volunteer at seven times that, no organization monitors or publishes the value of a nonprofit board member. One could extrapolate that the value of a nonprofit board member's seventy-five to one hundred and twenty hours of annual service would be at least as much, if not more, than a skilled volunteer. This led Inspiring Service to conclude that the annual value of a nonprofit board member is very conservatively estimated at ten thousand dollars per year, or thirty thousand dollars over the average three-year board member commitment.

With an average size community potentially achieving one hundred new board placements each year, a robust board-matching process would yield a three million-dollar economic value for a community. But instead, because of the sudden and severe disruption the pandemic caused, the focus of community leaders quickly turned to providing basic needs—food, shelter, and emergency services. The expansion of an innovation that would help create WIDER nonprofit boards—no matter how vital and how visionary—would have to wait.

But Inspiring Service didn't sit idly by.

While the pandemic and social unrest in 2020 forced communities to think less about the makeup of their nonprofit boards—freezing a national expansion—Inspiring Service's primary funder pushed the organization forward, introducing even more innovation around its board matching platform in its core communities.

The board matching platform works twenty-four seven. But Inspiring Service knew from its work with nonprofits that the demands on a nonprofit executive director's time makes it difficult for them to carve out even a fraction of time to devote to monitoring their dashboard and evaluating potential candidates inside the platform.

Likewise, prospective volunteer board leaders tend to be the most active members of a community, busy with their professional and personal lives. The action of pursuing additional board positions can easily fall from one's daily, monthly, or even annual list of priorities without a tool that makes it easy.

These facts prompted Inspiring Service to create an event driven by the algorithm matching, offering an opportunity for nonprofits and prospective volunteer leaders to connect with their best fits. The new technology makes the event more efficient than the old job fair model of bringing together in a hotel ballroom or some other facility a large group of interested leaders and nonprofits on the lookout for new board members. The technology curates for both the candidates and the nonprofits a prioritized list of people participating whom they should meet. Without that curation, the job fair model fails miserably.

Before and After

Before the pandemic, physical board-matching events across two communities—Cincinnati and Boston—produced more than seventy-five board placements under a model of two to three events per city per year. While you would expect the board-matching technology to assist smaller nonprofits without recruitment resources and private companies without the layers of management geared toward creating social responsibility opportunities for their senior leaders, the platform works for companies and nonprofits of *all* sizes.

For example, a BIPOC from Procter & Gamble Co. used the board-matching platform and event to discover his first board service opportunity. As an executive in a leadership role with a prominent company, he could certainly have chosen a board role with a well-known nonprofit. But he ended up connecting with a nonprofit he never would have found, thanks to Inspiring Service's innovative technology. These kinds of connections demonstrate the power of technology to help start relationships and to help nonprofits make greater strides toward fulfilling their missions.

It was the innovation around the event, as well as the use of artificial intelligence (the learning by machines of tasks previously only accomplished by humans) that prompted Independent Sector, Accenture, and the Chronicle of Philanthropy to award Inspiring Service with its "Innovate for Good" recognition in the program's second year.

After the pandemic hit, communities where the board-matching platform had already begun were eager to see the events continue. To meet this need, Inspiring Service converted the physical event to virtual. The virtual platform brought even greater ingenuity. With a single click, a candidate could schedule all their online meetings with their best fits among the nonprofits, further streamlining the connection process. While the world became accustomed to doing business and networking on platforms like Zoom, Inspiring Service created a much more user-friendly experience in moving from one meeting to another.

As appetites for returning to in-person events rise, the board-matching platform will likely evolve to a hybrid method. Many nonprofits and candidates appreciated the efficiency of the virtual events and will likely want to continue the time savings and lower participation barriers. Others may prefer in-person events. Fortunately, Inspiring Service can accommodate whichever method a person or organization prefers. This kind of resilience, flexibility, and adaptability is vital, and although it came about due to the pandemic, the changes are likely here to stay.

While continuing to nurture the board-matching platform, Inspiring Service expanded its board-matching algorithm to go back to its roots—matching skills-based volunteers with nonprofits who needed specialized help.

The ultimate skills-based volunteers, nonprofit board members across the country, began helping nonprofit leaders think through survival strategies. While some nonprofit boards were capable of providing strategic advice to navigate the unknowns caused by the devastating pandemic, most were not. Dire predictions suggested that 30 percent or more of the nation's nonprofits would fail.

Faced with ever-changing health and political landscapes that were making most organizations' strategic plans (and certainly their 2020 budgets) irrelevant, many for-profit leaders began to implement a more short-term planning model—a model not often used or discussed broadly in management circles. Around since the 1970s, "scenario planning" began to emerge as a critical tool to help organizations begin the process of sorting out how they could win when the circumstances were changing by the month, day, and even the hour. Seeing the success enjoyed by for-profits who used this model, nonprofits began adopting the approach as well.

Instead of a strategic plan's often two-, three-, or five-year gaze into what an organization would look like in the future, scenario planning is designed to help an organization think through the many paths it may encounter based on volatile outside factors. This method can help guide the organization's thinking based on any of a variety of potential outcomes. Scenario planning is especially useful in helping organizations avoid impulsive decisions that are typically made when leaders are reeling from crisis situations. Scenario planning helps eliminate the bias toward optimistic thinking seen in strategic planning and prepares an organization to be thoughtful about even those things that would seem unlikely to occur. Like a pandemic. Like George Floyd's murder. Like rioting in major cities. Like culture wars. Like the horrors at the Capitol on January 6, 2021.

Knowing what it knew about the active nonprofits in dozens of communities, Inspiring Service adjusted its board-matching algorithm and applied it to the skills nonprofits needed from volunteers to proceed with scenario planning. It began offering nonprofits the opportunity to be matched with purposefully constructed teams who wanted to help during a very difficult time for our nation but couldn't engage in their traditional ways because of the physical distancing restrictions of the pandemic.

As the world embraced virtual work, the process of creating a scenario plan moved online as well. Here's how it worked: After prospective skilled volunteers created profiles of themselves to match their interests and skills, the algorithm would recommend the best fits among the nonprofits who stepped forward to participate in the scenario planning-creation project. The platform was further adjusted to help create the best teams, whether the teams came from a single organization—like a company, service group, or membership association—or from a collective of general community volunteers not affiliated with any single organization. Then, to accelerate and customize the connections of the best fits even further, an online meetup would help the prospective volunteers get to know the nonprofits who were seeking help. Inspiring Service then used feedback from both the prospective volunteers and the nonprofits to create the best scenario planning team matches. As a result of the technology, the process a nonprofit would normally have to go through to create a scenario plan was shortened from months to a matter of weeks.

While there are two primary national websites that assist skills-based volunteers in connecting with nonprofits, neither focuses on helping skills-based volunteers connect with nonprofits in their own communities. And neither has achieved a scale that even begins to address the large market of people, especially younger generations, who embrace skills-based volunteering. Further, neither large national platform accommodates team projects.

Dozens of nonprofits took advantage of the scenario planning creation opportunities in 2020, and Inspiring Service found itself creating hundreds of thousands of dollars in impact in a new and powerful way. With an average scenario planning team consisting of five volunteers, contributing ten to fifteen hours of volunteer time each at an average rate of two hundred dollars per hour, a scenario planning exercise could easily exceed fifteen thousand dollars in value. A quarterly cycle of twenty projects results in over one million dollars in annual economic impact.

One company, PriceWaterhouseCoopers (PwC), fielded five teams, helping organizations that varied greatly in size, from a local YMCA to a regional foodbank to a small theater company:

"This was an excellent match, and I've heard so many impassioned stories from our assorted PwC team members about how this was special to each of them, and we are all proud of the collective impact, which was significant," said a PwC partner in charge of regional engagement.

As the fog begins to lift and we emerge from the darkest days of the pandemic, communities may be interested in embracing board-matching, and now the skills-based team connecting platforms. While Inspiring Service has continued to work with communities—some of the nation's largest like Boston and Los Angeles—it has also expanded its collaboration at the state level. This entails working with state service commissions, which exist in all but one of the nation's states. These service commissions are charged as nonprofits or state agencies and they help volunteers statewide address the issues that government and business leave to nonprofits to solve. Consider these examples:

- In Massachusetts, service commission leaders are working with local community leaders across the Commonwealth to provide tools that no single New England community could afford to build on their own.
- In Nevada, the state service commission has consolidated all of its connecting platforms, including the board-matching feature, on one website.

- Michigan continued its leadership in the sector in securing the largest Volunteer Generation Fund grant ever from AmeriCorps (formerly the Corporation for National and Community Service) to put Inspiring Service's platforms, including the board-matching and skills-matching portals, in place in Michigan.

Out of disruption have come smarter ideas, better implementation, and the development of more effective recruiting methods for getting citizens of our great nation to help nonprofits where they are needed the most.

The pandemic and social and political unrest of the last two years has made the "VUCA"—volatile, uncertain, complex, and ambiguous—world that futurist Bob Johansen described in his 2017 *New Leadership Literacies* book even more so.

Johansen wrote (well before the arrival of COVID-19 and long before the world had heard of George Floyd) that very little will remain constant in the next decade, and that with amplified digital connectivity, the speed, frequency, and scope of change will be dramatically different than anything we have ever experienced. Johansen also said that what can be distributed *will* be distributed.

Inspiring Service has created, tested, and implemented technology tools to better distribute volunteer recruitment. Now it is up to leaders of nonprofits, businesses, and government across our nation to be bold enough to embrace them.

If we are to continue to make progress, this work must continue, full speed ahead.

Students Self-Organize for Impact

Amay Aggarwal and Mary Zhu

Amay Aggarwal graduated from Stanford University in 2021, where he earned his M.S. in Computer Science and B.S. in Management Science and Engineering in four years. Amay has prior experience using Artificial Intelligence/Machine Learning and data science for social good and is primarily interested in using technology to aid low socio-economic areas. Born in India and having lived several years each in Singapore, the United Kingdom, New Zealand, and China, Amay enjoys traveling and learning different languages.

Mary Zhu graduated from Stanford University in 2021, where she earned both her B.S. and M.S. in Computer Science in four years. Born to immigrant parents in Wisconsin and raised in New Hampshire, Mary grew up receiving nonprofit aid and is particularly passionate about giving back and serving the economically disadvantaged. She founded her first nonprofit in high school and in 2021 delivered a talk at TEDxStanford on "Rethinking Volunteerism: Donating Your Comparative Advantage."

* * *

At 5:00 p.m. on Wednesday, March 18, 2020, thousands of students were forced to leave Stanford University to stem the coronavirus outbreak and adhere to Santa Clara County rules. We were only halfway through the third year of our undergraduate studies. Mary was heading thirty-two hundred miles back to New Hampshire, while Amay was flying halfway across the world to Auckland, New Zealand. Neither of us were certain of when we would return to Palo Alto, California. Not only were the student activities we both participated in getting cut, but we also started hearing from our peers that their internships were also being canceled and companies were instituting hiring freezes. The real-life experiences and relationships normally made through the preprofessional clubs and corporate internships—which play a vital role in a student's career trajectory—were being lost.

Old Websites Are No Longer Adequate

At the same time, we realized nonprofits across the country and around the world were also facing tremendous uncertainty and challenges. Volunteer opportunities and fundraising events were being canceled, funding priorities were being shifted to meet the greatest needs caused by the pandemic, and staff were being furloughed. Whereas an antiquated website might have been tolerable in normal times, it became devastating as the world turned virtual and organizations were forced to rely on their online presence to connect with beneficiaries, volunteers, and donors. Nonprofits needed to connect over the internet as much as any retailer. But tech talent has perpetually been expensive and hard to find, particularly for cash-strapped nonprofits.

After spotting these critical needs from both nonprofits and college students, we created Develop for Good. We pair and support university undergraduate and recent graduate volunteers as they design and develop tech products for nonprofits and governing agencies.

We decided to focus on websites, mobile apps, data analysis, and other design projects. To meet all our objectives, we realized we needed to build teams of students to work on the projects. The roles we created included designers, developers, data analysts, and product managers. This approach gave volunteers valuable real-world experience while delivering the best result for nonprofits; it kept everyone engaged while building new relationships during a time of isolation.

In April of 2020, after reaching out to some organizations to learn what they might need, we started with three projects. We began by disseminating the opportunities over Stanford University departmental mailing lists; consequently, our volunteer students were initially all from Stanford. But by the summer, an additional fifteen tech projects were getting started and interest had quickly grown well beyond Stanford. We were attracting students across the state from schools like University of California (UC)-Berkeley, UCLA, and USC, as well as nationwide at universities such as MIT, Brown, Cornell, and Columbia.

We started building teams to work with nonprofits of all sizes, from small organizations addressing timely issues to large organizations including UNICEF, the World Health Organization, the Smithsonian Institution, the World Bank, the Dana-Farber Cancer Institute, and the Environmental Defense Fund.

For example, a team of our developers created full-stack educational mobile and web applications for the more than one hundred-year-old global Save the Children young people's rights advocacy organization with the goal of connecting youth to employment opportunities and support services. Similarly, a team was creating an in-house mobile application to help serve families of hospitalized children with contact-free guest check-ins in light of COVID-19 for Ronald McDonald House Charities.

Resourcefulness Key To Startup

As an unstaffed start-up nonprofit, we needed to be very resourceful. We scoped each project to determine the technical skills that would be required. We created a Google form for volunteer applications. After reviewing all the applications, we used a Google spreadsheet to build teams composed of a product manager and developers and/or designers based on criteria like their experience and skills, time zones, and project interests. We emailed invitations to potential project team participants and awaited a returned commitment agreement. If we didn't receive it by the deadline, we replaced them with new members to the team. We created Slack channels for communication and utilized Notion—a note taking and task management software for project management—and monitored projects frequently to ensure they were progressing. All of this was maintained while we both continued college courses at Stanford online.

Before long, we also created an advisory board of industry experts. But as the fifteen projects of the summer grew to forty-five projects by the fall, we needed to establish a distributed leadership model to accommodate the growth. So, we built a volunteer leadership team; our Senior Executive Team included positions for Executive Directors, Marketing, Legal, Technology, Program, Design, Financial, and Community. We established additional Executive Team positions for Partnerships, Strategy, Design Projects, User Experience (UX), App Projects, Data, and more.

Volunteer Pathways Were Clear

We also built a clear path for volunteers to take on larger roles. Past project volunteers often become product managers in the next cycle. Past product managers could be promoted to managing directors overseeing three to five projects. And managing directors could take additional positions on the Executive Team. This distributed leadership model with upward mobility opportunities played a critical role in our ability to scale. It was also key to administrative sustainability as student leaders graduated and entered careers in industry.

By October 2020, we had over three hundred volunteers engaged in over forty-five projects. At this point, we had accumulated over twenty thousand hours of volunteer service, saving our nonprofits clients an estimated two million dollars in development costs. The press started to take notice throughout the fall and into the winter and were eager to share our story.

Articles in *TechCrunch, The Stanford Daily, CyberTalk* and others attracted more volunteers, which helped drive interest from people in industry. As more and more people with industry experience contacted us asking to help, we realized we didn't want to have them do technical work on the projects, as we intended that to be done by students or recent graduates. However, they *could* bring great value as industry mentors, providing advice to the product managers and project teams as needed. This way, we could engage more volunteers and produce even better results. Industry mentors came from Adobe, Airbnb, Amazon, Facebook, Google, LinkedIn, Microsoft, and more.

With more projects in the fall cycle, we could engage more volunteers. With more volunteers, we learned that a few people had to drop out because they were unable to work for free because they were experiencing financial stress within their own families. As a result, at the end of 2020, a major tech company sponsored a stipend for first-generation and low-income students to help defray the financial impact of volunteer work for some students.

Press Coverage Attracted Key Partnership

As the pandemic raged on, we received over one thousand volunteer applications to work on thirty-two projects in the January 2021 project cycle. Everything came into place. We matched over two hundred volunteers to teams with product managers and one or more industry mentors. Managing

Directors oversaw teams, and we added more community-building activities.

The resulting press coverage, as mentioned, created additional opportunities for partnerships. One of those partnerships was with another nonprofit who'd developed software for accepting and reviewing applications and building teams with diverse skills for projects. Starting with the Spring 2021 cycle, we no longer needed to use Google forms for applications and Google spreadsheets for building teams. Working together, we streamlined and updated many of the processes, creating the opportunity to engage more volunteers on more projects.

As we approached the summer 2021 project cycle, we knew there were still so many nonprofits who needed technology help, but we wondered if the students would be just as interested in volunteering as they were returning to school and internships. We were happy to discover that interest to do this meaningful type of volunteer work remains very high.

Develop for Good was created to address the disruption of internships and the heightened technology needs of nonprofits caused by the pandemic. Students in the fields of design, data analysis, and technology came together to address the immediate needs. What we created has potential well beyond just meeting those immediate needs.

As an organization, we now have a longer-term vision to provide meaningful opportunities and valuable team experiences to every student who wants them. To accomplish this, we are working on creating financial sustainability so that we can bring on the appropriate staff to insure our long-term stability and growth.

The Mentoring Field: A Lesson in Persistence and Evolution

Elizabeth Santiago, PhD, and David Shapiro

Elizabeth Santiago, PhD, is a Senior Advisor at MENTOR National where she formerly held the role of Chief Program Officer. While at MENTOR National, she was actively involved in the management of programs and services to support and build the mentoring field. She is most proud of her work focusing on racial equity and sharing power in the mentoring relationship as well as her work to elevate the importance of quality relationships for youth that specifically support building their networks and social capital. Currently, she is teaching creative writing courses at Boston College and Grub Street, working on a young adult novel to be released by Lee and Low in the fall of 2022, and building a website called The Untold Narratives (www.theuntoldnarratives.com). Liz earned a BFA in creative writing from Emerson College, a master's degree in education from Harvard University, and a PhD in education studies from Lesley University.

David Shapiro is CEO of MENTOR, the national organization unifying and elevating the mentoring movement through expertise, advocacy, and awareness. A servant leader in the field for more than fifteen years locally and nationally, David has dedicated his career to working across sectors and driving equity through the power of relationships. His movement-building expertise has been recognized by Social Impact Exchange, the *Stanford Social Innovation Review*, and Grantmakers for Effective Organizations. During Shapiro's leadership, MENTOR has partnered with leading brands including the NBA, Nike, Starbucks, LinkedIn, and Microsoft to expand mentoring through cause elevation, grown its national footprint to include twenty-four affiliates nationwide providing on the ground expertise, and worked extensively with the Obama Foundation to center mentoring through My Brother's Keeper Alliance. Additionally, MENTOR was selected by the U.S. Office of Juvenile Justice and Delinquency Prevention to create and operate the National Mentoring Resource Center.

"I'm thankful for technology during this time, but I also think it puts a spotlight on new forms of mentoring that need to be developed. In-person mentoring [...] isn't the norm anymore. The more challenges are introduced, the more ways we need to evolve."
—A volunteer mentor during the pandemic

COVID-19 has not only taken a devastating toll on physical health, but also on the overall well-being of too many. It has caused the loss of life, job loss, food insecurities, childcare issues due to cancellation of in-person activities, and extensive stress, fear, and isolation. With the additional challenges the pandemic introduced, volunteer mentors and mentoring organizations had to adapt quickly to maintain much-needed social connection for young people as well as additional layers of family and community support.

During all of this, a resounding spotlight shone on persistent racial injustices represented most tragically in the collective witnessing of the deaths of George Floyd, Breonna Taylor, and Adam Toledo, to name just a few. Mentors, who are mostly volunteers, have had to adjust not only in the mediums in which they mentor, but also build their ability to better understand the condition and context of young people to best meet them where they are mentally.

Yet, despite this crisis, mentoring organizations persisted. They were not going to accept that mentoring relationships would simply have to pause for an indefinite amount of time. They asked for support in how to move their programming to a virtual platform so as not to lose valuable connection time. But moving to virtual methods was not simply about picking the right technology. The support they asked for centered around key questions like, how does a mentoring program ensure safety? How can they prepare mentors to leverage technology to build and maintain meaningful relationships? What if families couldn't access the technology tools needed to maintain connection? What about mental health challenges related to the pandemic? How were mentoring programs to prepare mentors for discussions related to the civil unrest happening in the country?

MENTOR, as the field leader, has had to pivot quickly to provide much-needed guidance, support, and resources to meet the overwhelming needs of the mentoring field and the families they serve. MENTOR is a national nonprofit created in 1990 to fuel the quality and quantity of mentors. We partner with an affiliate network comprised of organizations across the country who serve the local field and grow the movement. Together, we research best practices in mentoring, advocate for policies that support relationship-centered approaches, promote mentoring as a leading youth development strategy, and provide innovative training and technical assistance focused on quality mentoring and youth development.

In the weeks after COVID-related social distancing restrictions were first put in place, MENTOR conducted a survey of mentoring organizations nationwide to gauge the impact of the pandemic on mentoring and helped contribute to a larger national study of COVID-19 issues conducted by our partners at Pacific Market Research (PMR). In the PMR survey, we asked a large national sample of adults whether they mentored, the impact that the pandemic has had on these relationships, and the circumstances of the young people themselves.

Among those findings:

- About one third of mentors reported that the pandemic has led to a positive impact on their mentoring relationships, likely through more frequent check-ins and shifts in the types and amounts of support offered. One in five mentors reported spending more time together and offering increased support.
- However, a quarter of mentors reported that their relationships have been negatively impacted, mostly through program closures and suspended meeting times (29 percent of respondents).

- Videoconferencing and phone calls were the most common ways of meeting with mentees while physically apart, although one in three mentors reported meeting with their mentee in person while maintaining social distance.
- Almost half of all mentors reported that virtual mentoring meetings had been successful for them and their mentee.
- However, one in five mentors had *not* been in contact with their mentee since the pandemic hit.
- Eighty-three percent of respondents felt that schools need to expand the use of mentors to offer students increased support and offset the loss of instructional time and enrichment opportunities.

Qualitatively, we learned that programs were nervous about how to ensure young people had their basic needs met, how mentoring programs should adapt to accommodate the myriad of requests they were getting, and how to keep mentors engaged without overstepping safety boundaries.

Programs had to go beyond focusing on mentoring; as a result, volunteer mentors had to wear multiple hats. To continue reaching young people, programs had to adapt their offerings. This was especially urgent for us as a field because the youth we serve may have *already* been struggling with feelings of isolation and may have come to mentoring programs precisely because they needed supportive and individualized adult engagement.

Said a program administrator at a mentoring program in Nevada of its innovation, "We are offering Netflix watch parties, a yoga studio is doing Zoom classes, we did a Facebook Live cooking class, we are sharing other community Zoom and web-based classes. We are encouraging Facetime, texting, and mailing notes. Mentors can pick up school packets and food to drop off, with appropriate distancing, to their mentees."

Addressing the Needs While Leading the Field

At MENTOR, we have worked to support the field in several ways to ensure physical distance does not mean social disconnection. We were particularly concerned that our most vulnerable youth would not be able to connect with their mentors, and we coalesced with key partners around a solution. Partnering with e-mentoring leaders iCouldbe and CricketTogether, we offered the Virtual Mentoring Portals (VMP), which allows mentoring organizations to triage their mentoring matches on to a safe, content-rich, age-appropriate virtual platform to continue their relationships.

iCouldBe, one of the leading experts on virtual mentoring in the United States since 2000, offered their tool to provide unstructured (internal, monitored email) or structured (research-backed curriculum) communications for existing mentees ages thirteen or older, and their mentors. CricketTogether, a one-on-one e-mentoring program in existence since 2007, offered their tool to programs that serve existing matches ages twelve and under. Both platforms have been constructed with respect to best practices, safety, and data privacy.

MENTOR hosted webinars to promote the tools and inform mentoring organizations how to sign up. We also built a page on our website with tools and resources to support transitioning to virtual mentoring including best practices for engaging youth online. The response was overwhelming. To date, we have had over one thousand hours spent by over four hundred and fifty mentor-mentee match pairs utilize the VMP to stay connected.

Once we addressed the challenge of how to maintain much-needed human connections for young people, we began compiling and developing tools and resources to support the effects the pandemic had, and continues to have, on mental health. We began to fully build out a page on our website to address COVID-related challenges the mentoring field was facing and partnered more fully with the Office of Juvenile Justice and Delinquency Prevention in running the National Mentoring Resource Center (NMRC). The NMRC allows any mentoring program in the United States to apply for technical assistance at no charge to the program. We moved all technical assistance to a virtual delivery and ensured we had adequate tools and resources.

Witnessing the isolating mental health effects of the pandemic on students along with the proven positive impact of mentoring on youth well-being, the extraordinary investment in public education through the American Rescue Plan (ARP) provides opportunities to use these new tools, insights, and community-school partnerships to prioritize relationships for students. ARP was launched by the Biden administration to provide immediate relief to American workers who have been under financial hardship due to the aftereffects of the COVID-19 pandemic. We are calling for investment in collaboration, training, design, and coordination work to create relationship-centered schools.

The pandemic offered a more widespread window into inequities like the digital divide, but also the important intersections of mental health and home life for young people. With potentially transformational investments in everything from holistic community school models to social workers to digital infrastructure, local implementation will be key when it comes to leveraging, investing, and integrating nonprofits and volunteer forces. School districts must invest in coordinating and aligning community partnerships to jointly reach key outcomes not only in academics but in a way that is linked, far more holistically, to the overall well-being of our young people.

It was vital for us as a movement leader to also build off past work to further interrogate the racial inequities that have permeated the country and our field. During the pandemic, MENTOR, in partnership with Youth Mentoring Action Network, a mentoring and youth development program in Ontario, California, cohosted the Black Youth Town Hall, a youth-led community dialogue aimed at supporting young people as they process events happening around them and to hear from them about the supports needed from mentors and the mentoring field. We had over three hundred participants from the United States and U.K. join the event.

But we knew that the issues facing our country are not the sole responsibility of young people. MENTOR New York coalesced leaders from our affiliate network and hosted a discussion called *Leading with Intention in the Fight for Racial Justice: MENTOR Affiliate Leaders Look Within the Movement* that held a spotlight to the work being done on the ground to support racial justice and the issues still plaguing the field.

To show solidarity and commitment to disrupting systems, a group of white leaders—comprised of MENTOR National and Affiliate staff from Colorado and Rhode Island along with program leaders from across the country—hosted an event titled, "Driving Equity in Mentoring: What White Leaders are Learning and Unlearning." These discussions are just the beginning in the acceleration of a long-term shift needed in our movement.

Persistence and Evolution

"Mentoring during this time is a unique and rewarding challenge [...] it is offering an opportunity to self-assess while assessing the needs of those I serve. In this season of life, human connections are being strengthened like never before. I count it as an honor and a privilege to serve at a time like this."

—A volunteer mentor during the pandemic*

Having been through the first phases of this pandemic, many truths became evident. First, mentoring organizations quickly realized technology's unique benefits—such as using the power of technology to match mentor-mentee pairs, training volunteers on a larger, more frequent scale, transcending time zones and transportation restrictions to connect with hard-to-reach youth, and providing longitudinal data on student support.

iCouldBe's Executive Director Kate Schrauth says the rise in e-mentoring interest was an ideal opportunity for iCouldBe

---

* Michelle Kaufman et al., "Mentoring in the time of COVID-19: Online Discussions with Mentors to Youth." *American Journal of Community Psychology*, (July 2021): https://doi.org/10.1002/ajcp.12543.

to learn from practitioners. "The consultation process with these organizations was an incredible moment to be active listeners—to increase engagement and achieve better outcomes," she says. "A workplace mentoring program that before the pandemic was meeting eight times a year was now meeting weekly, and programs that used to meet to snowboard and surf were still able to connect and build relationships and measure outcomes in new, dynamic ways."

E-mentoring Now A Long-Term Strategy

And even with the return of in-person connections, e-mentoring is here to stay because of its flexibility. "I think the most stunning outcome," says Schrauth, "is that all of these organizations see virtual mentoring as part of their long-term strategy."

The actionable data that is available on virtual mentoring platforms is another key reason why organizations are staying with an online component. Real-time information about user engagement—such as activities completed, average number of words posted per activity by mentees and mentors, and the ratio of mentee to mentor posts—provide important indicators about relationship development and mentee engagement.

On the platform, users can access tables and charts that display color-coded scores to help staff, teachers, and administrators easily identify matches with low engagement who need support or intervention as well as those with high engagement to celebrate.

"This data is a game-changer for relationship-centered schools," says Schrauth. "In a postpandemic world, we will see more and more blended mentoring models. And with the data, we will see relationships are going to be deeper and stronger."

While mentoring organizations are reimagining their recruitment, matching, and training processes in light of more technology use, MENTOR* is committed to researching the practices and structures that drive impact when leveraging virtual mentoring so we may utilize technology in the most effective ways. While technology won't ever fully replace in-person, human connection, the pandemic has proven that it does indeed have a place and a tremendous value.

Our racial equity work will be ongoing. While we continue to work on ourselves as individuals who carry bias that can potentially perpetuate inequities, work on our organizations to support interrogating practices that lead to injustice and work with the field combatting ideas of white saviorism that can harm communities, MENTOR has also partnered to expand on burgeoning work with the Center for Critical Mentoring and Youth Work to bring Critical Mentoring, which is mentoring that is designed to elevate youth voice and support the critical analysis of the context in which youth live in order to support youth in ways that are healing and empowering. This partnership will result in intensive training for our affiliates across the country for them to support local mentoring programs in being antiracist organizations. As field leaders, we must not just talk the talk, but also walk the walk. This work is also rippling out

---

* MENTOR: The National Mentoring Partnership, "Findings from MENTOR's Research into the Impact of COVID-19 on Mentoring Programs and Relationships," MENTOR, 2020, https://www.mentoring.org/wp-content/uploads/2020/08/Findings-from-MENTOR's-Research-Into-the-Impact-of-COVID-19-on-Mentoring-Programs-and-Relationships.pdf.

in our ability to invest in innovative work of our affiliates to progress in centering on mentoring for racial equity and to work with employers' relationship-centered practices to drive equity in hiring, retention, and pathways.

The big questions are, can the mentoring field go back to how it used to be? And should we go back? The quick answer is, we cannot, and we must not.

Resilience, persistence, and ingenuity have guided the mentoring field as we've faced the pandemic thus far. Moving forward, we must ensure continued innovation and, we hope, continued evolution.

Redefining Community in a Hybrid World

Beth Steinhorn

As president of VQ Volunteer Strategies, **Beth Steinhorn** partners with organizations and their leadership to increase impact through strategic and innovative volunteer engagement. Beth has authored multiple books and articles on strategic volunteer engagement and helped found The National Alliance for Volunteer Engagement to advance the national dialogue about volunteerism and engagement. Prior to becoming a consultant, Beth worked as an executive director and marketing director with education and faith-based organizations and spent years working with museums as an educator, manager, and anthropologist. She draws upon her anthropology experience still, helping organizations shift their culture to embrace volunteer engagement as a strategy to fulfill mission.

* * *

Like so many of my colleagues, when I think back to the years I spent as a staff member in nonprofits—first in museums and then in other education organizations—what stands out for me are the wonderful people with whom I was privileged to work. Both paid staff and volunteers. My team. But it was more than just a team—considering the number of holidays we celebrated together (sometimes at the museum when working on Thanksgiving, and sometimes offsite on personal time), exciting lifecycle events we shared, and, yes, funerals we attended, they were my *community*. A community that was nurtured by traditional events like volunteer potlucks and group field trips—but created out of shared values, a cause we all cared about, the chance to grow together, and the confidence that we were there for each other if needed.

The Power of Community

Yet, when health concerns arose due to COVID-19 and organizations were forced to cancel the potlucks, rethink the recognition lunches, and miss out on the informal yet vitally important "water cooler conversations," many recognized that our physical health was not the only thing at risk. Our community—and the sense of belonging and purpose embedded in that—was also in peril.

As leaders of volunteers partnered with their colleagues in departments to reengineer their service delivery model—whether developing virtual tours by museum docents, connecting volunteers with neighbors to shovel walkways or do errands, or standing up new volunteer medical advisory teams—they also faced the concurrent challenge of figuring out how to sustain a sense of community among a corps of volunteers who were now working remotely when, prior to COVID-19, most community-building efforts relied on in-person gathering.

For many volunteers, community isn't just "nice to have," it's a motivator that drives people to serve. Of course, highest on the motivation list is to make a difference for a cause they care about. But not far behind is the chance to be part of a community. According to research by VolunteerMatch (a nonprofit dedicated to connecting prospective volunteers to opportunities to serve) and Sterling Volunteers (a platform that provides background checks on prospective volunteers to help organizations mitigate risk),[*] when volunteers were asked what motivates them to serve, 83 percent of volunteers reported "making an impact" but among the other top reasons were "being social and productive at the same time," "spending quality time with family and friends," and "bonding time with coworkers."

Being social, spending time with others, and bonding certainly speak to volunteers' interest in community—and volunteer engagement professionals know that. So, it is no surprise that when many organizations had to suspend volunteer activities or transition them to remote in response to the pandemic, one question I repeatedly heard was, "How can I sustain or create a sense of community among volunteers during these tough times?"

For organizations like Cornerstone Visiting Nurse Association (Cornerstone VNA), based in Rochester, New Hampshire, this question was especially relevant as community building was always part of Cornerstone VNA's strategy. Aside from office volunteers and board members, many roles for

---

[*] Sterling Volunteers and VolunteerMatch, "Industry Insights Nonprofit and Volunteer Perspectives," Sterling Volunteers, September 22, 2021, https://www.sterlingvolunteers.com/blog/2021/09/2021-industry-insights-nonprofit-and-volunteer-perspectives/.

this home, health, and hospice organization were, by nature, primarily solo endeavors. Pet companion volunteers, hospice volunteers, and senior companions traditionally go alone to a patient's home and connect with an older adult one on one. To balance the solitary nature of this volunteer work, Cornerstone VNA staff was dedicated to nurturing a sense of community. In-service learning programs and volunteer appreciation events were just a few of the ways that Cornerstone VNA volunteers gathered, learned together, celebrated together—and reinforced their communal identity. But, of course, those in-person activities were put on hold in the spring of 2020. Instead, Cornerstone VNA staff was forced to rethink and reinvent community-building strategies that could knit a collection of individuals together despite serving in disparate locations.

Keeping Communities Connected

Cornerstone VNA was not alone in this challenge, of course. For organizations like museums whose onsite operations were suspended, and volunteer activities significantly curtailed, leaders of volunteers sought to sustain relationships with and among volunteers. This would increase the chances of retention once volunteer activities could resume. At the same time, others encountered a different challenge. Food pantries, senior service organizations, and workforce development agencies faced dramatic increases in demand for services yet had many long-time volunteers choosing to serve only remotely (or not at all) because they were, themselves, at-risk. With new volunteers recruited to fill the gaps, volunteer engagement professionals anticipated rifts between the "veterans" and the "newbies." For them, building community was prioritized to ensure everyone cooperated and got the work done.

Regardless of the specifics, all my colleagues who sought to sustain a sense of community shared one motivation: They did so simply because *they cared*. In fact, it is "caring" that is a hallmark of communities.

According to researcher Charles Vogl, community is "a group of people who share mutual concern for one another."* In other words, members of community believe that other members care about them. Vogl also identified principles that characterize healthy, functioning communities. Those characteristics are clear boundaries that mark when a person has become part of the community, initiation into the group, symbols and rituals that represent the ideas that have meaning for the community, a space set aside for the community to engage with each other, stories that communicate the values of the corps, and pathways to grow as community members and leaders.

As Cornerstone VNA and others adapted their practices to sustain communities, they employed both proven practices and innovations and, whether knowingly or not, they tapped into the principles of effective communities.

The efforts, however, still beg the questions. Why should organizations even take the time to build community? With so many other priorities and challenges, what is gained by nurturing a community of volunteers? Vogl's research† revealed that when leaders build stronger communities, the communities are better positioned to:

---

*   Charles Vogl, *The Art of Community*, (Penguin Random House: 2016).

†   Charles Vogl, *The Art of Community*.

1. Help members grow in the ways they hope to.
2. Cause members to feel more connected, welcome, proud, and excited be part of the group.
3. Help members work together toward making the difference they envision.
4. Make being part of the community more fun.

Aren't these four things exactly what we want volunteers to achieve? Helping volunteers to find fulfillment and personal growth. Inspiring volunteers to be proud of their work and share that excitement with others, potentially recruiting others to contribute as well. Collaborating with other volunteers and staff to achieve mission. And, yes, to have fun while doing it.

Cornerstone VNA Embraced Community

Founded in 1913, Cornerstone VNA is an independent nonprofit organization providing home care, hospice, palliative care, private duty, and community services. Serving New Hampshire and Maine, their mission is to promote the optimum level of well-being, independence, and dignity of those living in the community by providing trusted, compassionate, and expert health care. Volunteers have been crucial to Cornerstone VNA's work throughout its history.

As the pandemic unleashed health concerns and strict protocols were instituted, Cornerstone VNA was forced to shut down all volunteer activities and shift services to virtual from March through June 2020. But, by summer, working with its emergency response coordinator to establish protocols, volunteers who were ready and felt comfortable returning were welcomed back. To ensure they could still provide comfort and companionship to community members in need, Cornerstone VNA created new volunteer positions and activities, like checking in by telephone with patients and their families, serving as patient pen pals, and even singing over the phone to provide comfort and trigger positive memories.

With many volunteers on hiatus and new opportunities emerging, Cornerstone VNA developed revised recruitment materials and welcomed new volunteers into the fold. In doing so, they implemented the first two of Vogl's principles of community—boundaries and initiation. Effective communities establish clear lines between who are members and who are nonmembers—not with the goal of keeping people out, but rather to ensure that those who cross the boundary into the community know that they are, in fact, "in." Initiations mark the transition over the boundaries, and, for volunteers, initiation comes in the form of background checks, training, an orientation and a special welcome from leadership, and, of course, their official badge. Even with activities being predominantly remote, when volunteers receive their Cornerstone VNA badge, they know they are officially and formally a part of this volunteer society.

While one might not normally associate symbols and rituals with volunteer engagement, symbols and rituals are objects and activities that bring meaning to an occasion—and volunteering often incorporates various meaningful occasions. Rituals may mark when a volunteer completes training, wraps up a project, or reaches a noteworthy tenure of service, whether one year or ten! Many organizations recognize that even the weekly gathering of the same team of volunteers before a shift at a museum or animal rescue organization, for example, was ritualistic—and volunteers *missed* it. I know of countless organizations that encouraged volunteer teams to convene virtually at the same time each week as their previously scheduled onsite shift. Using the organization's online meeting platform, these volunteers were able to sustain their team by connecting, catching up, and receiving updates on the organization's recovery, even when not gathering in person.

Naturally, Vogl's principle of having a dedicated space—a place for community members to convene and engage together—was among the most disrupted and transformed by COVID-19. No surprise, new virtual spaces were developed. Like so many others, Cornerstone VNA volunteers became accustomed to convening online for training, informal check-ins, and formal recognition celebrations.

Instead of in-person appreciation events, they sent letters of appreciation and assembled appreciation bags with fun gifts as a show of gratitude. They also delivered projects to volunteers' homes so that the volunteers could still complete them, though remotely. In the works is a new Facebook page for volunteers to get news and communicate with each other. But, amid the pandemic, Cornerstone VNA was also undergoing capital renovations and the volunteer engagement team advocated for a space dedicated for volunteers to work, gather informally, and store their personal items while volunteering. This area—known as "The Volunteer Hub" now complete with workspaces and volunteer cubbies—confirms to volunteers that they are valued and that their activities are worthy of a dedicated space.

Stories are a community's way to communicate values to itself and others. For Cornerstone VNA, email updates share new policies and protocols, spotlight the variety of volunteer roles, and highlight patient stories. In addition, the Spirit of NH award, organized by VolunteerNH (New Hampshire's state service commission) gave a chance to shine a light, albeit virtual, on the extraordinary efforts of companion volunteers and community mask-maker volunteers who were honored with the 2021 Cornerstone Award for their generosity in making and donating thousands of masks for the Cornerstone VNA community.

But, even more important, these updates and awards signal to all volunteers—whether active or still on hold—that they remain a part of this community throughout these challenging times. In their community building efforts, Cornerstone VNA also has been very clear that the community is not made up of just volunteers, rather it's the Cornerstone VNA community. Whether staff or volunteers, paid or unpaid, *everyone* committed to the Cornerstone VNA mission is part of the community. As the adage states, "information is power," and when it comes to community-building, having the "insider" information reinforces one's feeling of belonging and legitimacy within the community. Sharing organizational information with volunteers and staff breaks down the barriers between the two groups and reinforces their partnership.

Finally, leadership pathways which, for Cornerstone VNA, are intertwined with rituals, as volunteers are traditionally involved in memorial services for patients who have died. In shifting to virtual, Cornerstone not only invited volunteers to participate in virtual services but, in fact, empowered teams of volunteers to create *new* rituals so that they and the community at large could convene and pay tribute to the community member who had passed away. Volunteer leaders facilitate the memorial and arrange for a display of decorative butterflies as a moving symbol for the moment.

Make Intentionality Part of Your Strategy

Thanks to the efforts of leadership, the Cornerstone VNA volunteer community still thrives, as evidenced by the volunteers' satisfaction and continued service, and through the care and comfort provided to community members in need. Volunteer communities can thrive in person, virtually, or hybrid. But they will not thrive—nor will they reap the benefits of growth, connection, productivity, and even fun—if they are not nurtured intentionally.

This intentionality can become a part of your engagement strategy as well. To build or sustain a sense of community in this ever-changing world of volunteer engagement, take time to:

- Envision the type of community you seek to create.
- Integrate symbols, stories, and rituals that demonstrate the values that guide your mission.
- Remember that community includes both staff and volunteers, so it may be time to break down some of those age-old barriers between the two.
- Remember: Don't do this alone. Engage others with you in your community-building tactics. By partnering with others, you will lead authentically and strengthen the community for greater impact.

Rethinking Impact

Purpose-Driven Volunteer Impact

Sue Carter Kahl, PhD

Sue Carter Kahl is the President of Sue Carter Kahl Consulting and has spent her career in the nonprofit and philanthropic sectors. Her work is infused with lessons learned as a volunteer center executive, state service commissioner, nonprofit board member, staff member, volunteer, and researcher. Her current projects include consulting and training on the value that volunteers bring to organizations, translating research on volunteer impact into practitioner-friendly resources, and blogging at VolunteerCommons.com. Sue has a PhD in leadership studies and is committed to bridging practice and academia in the volunteer field. She serves as a pro bono coach for nonprofit executives with Fieldstone Leadership Network San Diego.

* * *

There is a shift occurring in the understanding of volunteer impact. Two brief examples offer a glimpse of the change underway:

- Three weeks into the pandemic shutdown, the senior leadership team proposed laying off the Volunteer Director. With no volunteers serving and no hours accruing anytime soon, they questioned the value she contributed to the organization.

- The rapid shift to pandemic programming followed by the social unrest after George Floyd's murder compelled L.A. Works, a volunteer center, to rethink volunteer impact. It had typically defined success by the number of volunteers mobilized, hours served, and agency partners engaged. Yet they started to realize their impact was not just how much service they generated but the extent to which that service was inclusive. They wanted to expand beyond tallying project outputs so they could discover and share what service meant to the volunteers as individuals and to the city as a collective.

These examples demonstrate how the tried-and-true strategies for reporting volunteer impact are coming up short. They urge us to consider how we might take a more generative approach to volunteer impact.

After all, volunteers contribute to agencies' mission, fundraising, and outreach. Those who have a positive experience also leave with a greater sense of transparency and trust in the agencies they serve[*]. Leaders need these tangible and intangible contributions for their nonprofits to be successful. Yet, too

---

[*] Sue Carter Kahl, "Why Volunteers are Worth the Trouble," in Top 20 Ideas in *Volunteer Engagement for 2020*, edited by Erin Spink, 24. http://www. spinktank.

often, volunteers are considered "nice but not necessary"*—
their power reduced to a few statistics that tell us more about
their volume or tenure than their results.

The pandemic and renewed social justice movement have
revealed the shortcomings of a narrow view of volunteer
impact. Framing volunteer value as hours served or years
retained meant that some agencies could not envision a role
for volunteers or the Volunteer Director in a pandemic. Volunteers and their leaders were put on hiatus or dismissed rather
than engaged as problem-solvers or placed in new roles.

Other agencies came to the realization that these metrics
checked the box for a best practice or met the needs of external
partners, like funders. However, they demonstrated little about if
and how volunteers advanced the mission. Traditional statistics
did not reflect what mattered to program participants or help
staff make informed decisions about programs. COVID-19 and
a more widespread awareness of racism uncovered the limitations of industry standard statistics like volunteer numbers,
hours, financial value, and tenure. Yet, the lessons learned apply
in less dramatic organizational changes as well, such as when
programs are modified or new audiences are engaged.

From Best Practice to Purposeful Practice

Best practices support leaders in directing their time and teams.
Unfortunately, they are not a panacea. One of the problems with
best practices is that they offer an illusion of standardization in

---

* David Eisner et al, "The New Volunteer Workforce," *Stanford Social Innovation Review* (Winter 2009), http://www.ssireview.org/pdf/ TheNewVol-
unteerWorkforce.pdf.

a field and activity that are incredibly diverse. They suggest that one size fits all, whether an agency is a grassroots environmental group run entirely by volunteers or a multimillion-dollar social services agency with hundreds of paid staff.

There is certainly merit in referring to best practices and industry standard measures. For example, tracking volunteer numbers and hours can help determine how much labor it takes to complete a project or program. It indicates how many community members have been involved in and exposed to the mission. Assigning an hourly dollar value to service monetizes volunteer time so it can be used in financial statements and as an in-kind match for some grants. (The most commonly used rate is calculated annually by Independent Sector, a national membership organization that works to strengthen civil society across sectors.) Reporting on indicators that are recognized as the industry standard lends an air of legitimacy to agency efforts.

However, accepting a best practice or industry standard without examining if or how it aligns with organizational purpose can be problematic. Tracking numbers alone favors quantity over quality; it gives the impression that having volunteers is good and having more volunteers is better. As such, it can subtly redirect attention from focusing on how to partner with community volunteers to advance the mission to how to increase volunteer numbers (the volunteer version of mission drift). The emphasis on pricing volunteer hours or tracking volunteer retention can also obscure other volunteer-related data that can be valuable even if less familiar.

The alternative is to shift from best practice to purposeful practice. Instead of relying on how other organizations report

volunteer impact, leaders have an opportunity to customize their approach to one that aligns with the organization's
purpose. What is the organization trying to achieve? How are
volunteers influencing those achievements? What do volunteers uniquely contribute? Gaining clarity and alignment
on the answers to these questions is the first step toward a
purposeful approach to articulating volunteer impact.

From Ideas to Action

Let's revisit our agencies from the introduction. In the first
case, the leadership team equated the value of the volunteer
function with its physical presence and hourly output. After
all, that's what they reported in the board and annual reports.
No volunteers and no volunteer hours meant no need for a
Volunteer Director in a pandemic. Had the leadership team
understood the broader contributions of the volunteer team,
however, they might have come to a different conclusion.

For example, early in the pandemic, a youth literacy organization in San Diego moved its volunteer-run, classroom-based
program online. With many educators transitioning to online
distance learning, some volunteers were not familiar with or
comfortable using the technology needed to support virtual
programming. Others needed to take a step back to navigate
personal challenges with COVID-19. The Engagement Team
took the lead in finding ways to involve volunteers in a virtual
environment to support online program delivery. As a result,
a new group of people found their way to the organization
because they had unexpected time on their hands and wanted
to support their community. They loved that they could do

something meaningful from home. These volunteers were more diverse in age, ethnicity, professional background, and languages spoken than the traditional volunteers and brought valuable qualities to the program.

The volunteer methods and numbers for the organization changed during the transition period.

The Engagement Team continually made the case for prioritizing the agency's mission, values, and community over numbers of volunteers alone. As a result, the agency now boasts its most diverse volunteer corps to date. Due to the new volunteers, service hours actually increased. The retention numbers for classroom-based volunteers decreased significantly during the first year of the pandemic, but these same volunteers took it upon themselves to learn the necessary technology to support virtual learning and are resuming their roles moving forward. The volunteer numbers fluctuate because the agency is still navigating the return to in-person learning, but the mission and values (and volunteer department) are alive and well.

Another agency closed its doors for programming early on but wanted to maintain a connection to its volunteers. An important part of its vision serving the LGBTQ community was to make every person feel welcomed, valued, and supported. To help achieve that vision, the Volunteer Services Director, Charles Enciso, helped create a volunteer leadership group that identified and facilitated learning opportunities such as antiracism book clubs and movie watch parties. Volunteers and staff participated. In fact, the opportunities for learning among volunteers even outpaced staff at times. Volunteers gained valuable learning and met other team members— and their training hours counted as service. Redefining what volunteering entailed meant that volunteer numbers remained high. Yet, it was not the number of hours that mattered per se, but what those hours represented: a way to maintain a sense of community and grow into the agency's vision.

In the final example, L.A. Works's internal discussions and work with an equity consultant revealed how they could mitigate unhealthy power dynamics in volunteer engagement. Going forward, the team committed to facilitating group volunteer projects that met the needs of everyone involved, not just corporate partners and volunteers. They identified the opportunity to coach their partner agencies in this work as well. It's an ongoing process, but so far, they are assessing and aligning internal projects with their values and a new equity framework. The next step is to help external partners do the same. These practices take more time than business as usual. They understand their numbers might decline. However, their dedication to living their values means that the service experience and action it inspires matters at least as much as the amount of service completed.

Disruption Brings Fresh Perspectives

If there is a silver lining in the pandemic and the renewed emphasis on race inequity, it may be that it is challenging assumptions about how volunteer engagement works in general and how we approach volunteer impact in specific. Though the disruption is unsettling, it allows us to bring fresh eyes to our work and try new strategies. Here are a few suggestions for experimenting with volunteer impact:

- **Align Impact Data with Purpose:** If an agency invests time and energy in involving volunteers, those volunteers should be helping to advance programs and operations. If volunteers are advancing programs and operations, there should be data that reflect their involvement. Taking this approach to identifying volunteer value indicators ensures that volunteer data points align with organizational data. When there is a disconnect between the two, it becomes much harder to justify investing in the volunteer function. Paint a picture of how volunteers contribute to the organization's success. Report on volunteer roles that support the organization's effectiveness.

- **Select Impact Data from the Inside Out:** Many nonprofits track data based on what funders or external partners require. However, these data points may not reflect what matters to those closest to the mission. Whereas a funder may care about numbers of volunteer hours and participants, the participants are likely more concerned with if the volunteers were caring and treated them with dignity. The volunteers probably want to feel like their time is respected and well spent. Starting with the opinions of those closest to the mission and volunteer experience provides a purposeful way to define impact. Inviting participants, participants' loved ones, volunteers, and/or staff into the conversation about volunteer impact assures that indicators are meaningful and relevant to them.

- **Take Best Practices with a Grain of Salt:** Just because a practice has been labeled "best" does not mean it universally applies to all nonprofits*. In fact, Hager and Brudney† determined that following best practices in volunteer management did not yield consistent positive outcomes across diverse organizations. They recommended that leaders "determine whether, how, and where these practices may work in their specific organizational circumstances, and adopt, adapt, or even discard them accordingly."

- **Watch your Language:** Language influences actions and can inadvertently narrow how we define impact. For example, it is common to talk about *measuring* impact. Unfortunately, *measuring* frames impact in terms of numbers only. Numbers work well when counting and pricing widgets. They can be poorly suited, however, for illuminating the complexity of nonprofit work, which deals with humans and transformation. Instead, it is more expansive to talk about *capturing* or *revealing,* instead of *measuring.* Likewise, *indicators, data, evidence,* or *information* are more inclusive of qualitative outcomes than *measures* or *metrics.* Broaden your language to enlarge your mindset.

- **Expand From Volunteer Value to Volunteer Worth:** On a related note, *worth* is more potent and relevant in

---

*   Robert D. Herman and David O. Renz, "Advancing Nonprofit Organizational Effectiveness Research and Theories: Nine Theses," *Nonprofit Management and Leadership* 18, no. 4 (Summer 2008): 399–415. https://doi.org/10.1002/nml.195.

†   Mark A. Hager and Jeffrey L. Brudney, "In Search of Strategy: Universalistic, Contingent, and Configurational Adoption of Volunteer Management Practices," *Nonprofit Management and Leadership* 25, no. 3 (Spring 2015): 235–254. https://doi.org/10.1002/nml.21123.

volunteerism than *value*. *Value* is a business term and suggests a price set by the market. *Worth* is more comprehensive. It includes material value, but it can also be imbued with meaning, sentiment, and tradition. It reflects not only the item or time given but the relationship between those in the exchange*. Because volunteerism is a gift of time and talent that is steeped in meaning and purpose, *worth* is a fuller and more accurate term than *value*. Embracing *worth* gives us permission to share stories and testimonials about the aspects of service that don't lend themselves to counting and to report the ways that service impacts the agency, volunteer, and community at large.

Though 2020 was disruptive, it was also enlightening. It helped reveal assumptions and values that are embedded in the nonprofit sector. It provided an opening and opportunity for us to question if those assumptions and values serve our communities and our organizations. And though the answers may still be unclear, the power of asking the right questions will remain with us for a long time.

---

*   Marcel Mauss, Essai sur le Don, trans. W. D. Halls (London: Alfred A. Knopf, 1990). Original work published 1950."

The Multifaceted Impacts of Service

Kaira Esgate

Kaira Esgate serves as the Chief Executive Officer of America's Service Commissions (ASC), the national association of the fifty-two state and territorial service commissions. ASC leads efforts to engage all states and territories in embracing service as a strategy to build community in solving local challenges through AmeriCorps and other national service programming. Prior to her current role, Kaira was the executive director of Reimagining Service, a national multisector coalition dedicated to converting good intentions to greater impact through effective volunteer engagement strategies. With Reimagining Service, Kaira led efforts to bring new data and insights to volunteering and developed the nationally recognized nonprofit service enterprise model. During her tenure with California Volunteers, the state service commission in California, Kaira served in a variety of roles, including as Chief of Staff to the nation's first Cabinet-level Secretary of Service and Volunteering.

* * *

Each morning, Mercedes serves as an Agriculture Assistant through AmeriCorps at Three Rivers Christian School in Cowlitz County, Washington, which, with nearly one in five residents experiencing food insecurity, has been hit hard by the COVID-19 crisis.

Across the country in Boston, Massachusetts, another Ameri-Corps member, Paloma, was serving with Social Capital Inc. at South End Community Health Center to create wellness programs when the COVID-19 pandemic began. With a master's degree in public health, Paloma screened 70 percent of the health center's patients to determine their needs in the early months of the COVID-19 pandemic—and continues to help fill those needs, arranging for meal distribution, setting up appointments for food and diaper pick-ups, and providing comfort to struggling families.

Meanwhile, from his home in Fort Collins, Colorado, Lance spent his days on the phone talking to people who had contracted the virus and others who were potentially exposed, sharing resources on care and information on how to quarantine effectively. As an AmeriCorps member with Colorado's COVID-19 Containment Response Corps, he worked with hundreds of other service members across Colorado to mitigate the spread of the disease.

Mercedes, Paloma, and Lance are part of national or state service programs, working to help the communities where they serve. National and state service programs, led federally by the AmeriCorps agency and locally by state service commissions, enable citizens to dedicate a year of their lives to service, helping to improve lives, foster civic engagement, and strengthen communities. The system is made possible through federal and state funds and the partnership of local host sites—organizations that share in the cost of living expenses and training provided to service members.

In addition to helping communities, service members also benefit from professional development, which, in turn, prepares a workforce for the nonprofit and public sectors. This threefold approach to service is part of what makes national and state service so unique—it is designed to address vital community needs such as food insecurity and urban safety, provide service members with meaningful skills, education, and experiences, and strengthen the public sector by developing a pipeline of future professionals. As in so many areas, COVID-19 both challenged and accelerated the work to achieve these intended impacts.

Disrupting the Model

Due to the COVID-19 pandemic and its associated restrictions, all three of these impact arenas were disrupted to their cores. Communities experienced increases in food insecurity and poverty, wider gaps in education, and, of course, the need to mitigate the spread of COVID-19 while caring for those affected by it. The pandemic also revealed and exacerbated inequities in American society; people of color were disproportionately affected by the public health and economic fallout of the pandemic.* Current members' limited income meant

---

* University of Washington, "2020 Washington State Food Security Survey," https://foodsystems.wsu.edu/wa-food-security-survey-and-report/.

they often faced food insecurity themselves, while prospective members were losing employment and having educational opportunities interrupted.

In terms of the talent pipeline for the nonprofit and public sectors, many leaders recognized the need for skilled team members due to ongoing budget shortages and a generation of retiring leaders. But once the pandemic hit, organizations faced a more pressing crisis: nonprofits, government agencies, and schools were challenged to deliver services amid the restrictions, some shifting to virtual and others suspending services entirely.

Nearly all these organizations traditionally achieve mission through in-person services, yet, overnight, were forced to completely rethink service models even among those that were simultaneously experiencing dramatic increases in demand. Not only were they challenged to think about a future talent pipeline, but their current staff were forced to adapt simply to keep their doors open and didn't necessarily have the skills to do so. Their teams needed development and increased capacity as soon as possible.

New Strategies to Drive Impact

Disruption-Driven Innovations

Throughout the nation, state service commissions looked to national service and their own state service initiatives as vital resources to address the emerging needs created or exacerbated by the crisis. In some cases, existing service programs were adapted in response, while in others, entirely new corps were developed. Regardless of approach, all had to keep in mind the multifaceted impacts that their programs are designed to accomplish—balancing community needs, member development, and helping to fuel a sustainable talent pipeline for organizations. It was—and remains—the ultimate in "building a bridge while crossing it," though, in this case, one might say that service commissions were building *three* bridges while crossing them!

Community Needs

In spring 2020, Colorado leaders sought to control the spread of COVID-19 and recognized that additional resources were needed. To provide extra support to local public health agencies, they created the COVID-19 Containment Response Corps (CCRC) as an innovative public-private partnership between AmeriCorps, the Polis-Primavera administration, the Serve Colorado state commission, Gary Community Investments, and the Colorado Department of Public Health and Environment. Four nonprofit partners* recruited and placed CCRC AmeriCorps members to support case investigation, contact tracing, resource coordination, test result notification, and quarantine monitoring to contain the spread of COVID-19.

The impacts on the community have been notable. In the first year alone, more than nine hundred AmeriCorps members provided support services to sixty thousand Coloradans, and members remained on the ground assisting the state with vaccine outreach and data collection needs in rural

---

* The four partners were Community Resource Center, Conservation Legacy, Cultivate, and Volunteers of America Colorado.

and urban areas. In addition to the quick response nature of this innovative program, two other aspects set this strategy apart. First, all service members operate remotely, helping to develop a highly diverse and intergenerational corps from all parts of the state—able to reach and support Coloradans wherever they live.

Second, the program is the result of an unprecedented level of collaboration. Each partner brought unique strengths to the initiative. The AmeriCorps agency and its partner nonprofits had disaster response experience and the systems to quickly deploy and support members. Serve Colorado's connection to the state government helped spread information about the initiative and recruit AmeriCorps members quickly. Gary Community Investments and private philanthropy helped provide the technology that members needed to serve virtually. Furthermore, AmeriCorps members hailed from all "streams of service" (namely, AmeriCorps State and National, VISTA, NCCC, and AmeriCorps Seniors). Although many of the partners had worked together on other initiatives, never had they worked together so quickly or closely. The unprecedented urgency of the COVID-19 pandemic removed barriers that had previously stifled collaboration and, instead, increased trust among partners as everyone was clearly working toward the same goal—saving lives across their state. As a result of this unique partnership, the CCRC became an integral part of Colorado's COVID-19 response.

The quick response and unprecedented partnership were not without challenges—communications among them. But the urgency of the crisis contributed to expedient solutions. Clarifying roles and expectations was essential. Once operational, all partners developed effective ways to communicate within their organization and with all external partners, ensuring that the program met community needs.

Member Development

While Colorado was standing up its CCRC, Washington State was also developing a cross-program corps to address the dramatic increase in food insecurity and the marked increase in youth unemployment. Early in the pandemic, one in three Washingtonians (approximately 2.2 million children and adults) lacked access to adequate food, with persons of color one and a half times more likely to be food insecure than white people. Additionally, unemployment for youth in Seattle was triple the rates pre-COVID.[*]

Serve Washington sought to address the loss of employment among young people and respond to the food insecurity crisis. To help do all that, it was important to further diversify the corps to better reflect the income and racial composition of communities served and remove possible access barriers for potential service sites and members. Consequently, the WA COVID Response Corps was formed in partnership with the Schultz Family Foundation to provide wraparound services for members, such as increased training, increased living allowances, and an emergency assistance fund for service members who needed it.

---

[*] Data dashboard - Mathematica. (n.d.). *Youth unemployment tracker*. Mathematica. Retrieved January 12, 2022, from https://www.mathematica.org/dataviz/youth-unemployment-tracker; and April 2021 report- Inanc, H. "Youth Unemployment in the First Year of the COVID-19 Pandemic: From the Breakout to the Vaccine Rollout." Cambridge, MA: Mathematica, April 2021.

In many instances, nonprofit organizations must pay host site fees in order to engage AmeriCorps members—this host fee often prevents small and/or under-resourced organizations from participating in AmeriCorps programming. As a result, subsidies for host site fees also made it easier for organizations to remain or become host sites. In fact, more than one-third of the host sites were first-time participants in AmeriCorps, and one-fourth would not have been able to participate without the foundation's fee contribution because of financial hardship.

While those tactics each mapped to specific goals, the effort was driven by something even bigger. Serve Washington Executive Director Amber Martin-Jahn explains, "We wanted to seize this opportunity to innovate, learn, and apply those lessons. Yes, this was about responding to COVID by leveraging national service, but it also was designed to address barriers to service that we have been hearing about from our programs and members."

And respond they did, with 125 service members providing food assistance to more than 2.27 million people across the state within the first nine and a half months of the COVID-19 pandemic. But the biggest innovations and learning came in member development, as Serve Washington worked to enact its vision of making service a mobility pathway for young people.

WA COVID Response Corps members received supplemental training, coaching, and post service transition advising. But some important lessons were learned along the way. While evaluations showed that the efforts provided a meaningful opportunity to many, some members also reported that it didn't really help them with their next career steps. Some members had already planned their next steps prior to starting service, while others found that the supplemental supports weren't customized enough to align with where they were in their education and career path.

These findings were powerful. In response, Serve Washington has modified member development for the 2021–22 WA COVID Response Corps cohort to focus on supporting individual members' current motivations and future career plans.

The increase in member living allowances was also designed to position service as an opportunity path for all. Results from the first cohort indicated that while such increases can reduce barriers to serving, they alone are not enough to achieve diversity-related goals. To increase diversity and recruit members from the communities being served, Serve Washington found that additional relationship building and localized community presence are needed—not just at recruitment time, but year-round. "To achieve that trust," Martin-Jahn explains, "Ameri-Corps rules and programs must offer flexibilities to support access to participation and member development and we must prioritize more investment in management, coaching, and wraparound services for members."

Building Organizational Capacity and Talent

The third of the multifaceted impacts for state and national service is strengthening organizations through a robust and sustainable talent pipeline—a goal that is naturally intertwined with others, especially providing service member development. While addressing community needs and member development are priorities of Massachusetts Service Alliance (MSA), when COVID-19 hit, MSA took a different approach than Colorado and Washington.

With the health-related response to COVID-19 being adequately addressed through community health agencies, MSA turned its focus to the pressing needs of the organizations serving existing needs across the state.

Moving from Future-Focused to the Here and Now

Throughout Massachusetts, organizations, including host sites for AmeriCorps and Commonwealth Corps (the state's service corps), had to shift their operating model from predominantly in-person to largely or entirely remote. Staff were struggling to sustain their services. Most organizations relied on volunteers before the pandemic and yet the restrictions severely curtailed their ability to engage volunteers to deliver on mission, whether aiding immigrants, tutoring students, providing companionship to seniors, or enriching the arts. While the goal of filling a talent pipeline is usually future-focused, the urgency of the pandemic changed all of that. MSA recognized that its constituent agencies were in peril, in immediate need of training and resources to pivot their practices, engage volunteers in new ways, develop an infrastructure to support these new ways of doing business, and learn from each other.

In response, MSA expanded professional development opportunities for staff and offered mini grants. State agencies were invited to participate in a well-curated training curriculum on volunteer engagement, including more than ten trainings for AmeriCorps members, technical assistance trainings for AmeriCorps program staff, and a robust virtual training calendar for nonprofits, including such topics as corporate partnerships, strengthening inclusion, purpose-driven volunteer impact, and harnessing volunteers to fuel recovery.

Meanwhile, the COVID-19 Resiliency Grant program, made possible through the AmeriCorps agency Volunteer Generation Fund and state commission funds, offered up to four thousand dollars per organization to support volunteer community service projects and volunteer capacity-building initiatives arising out of the COVID-19 pandemic. With more than one hundred fifty applications, it was clear that the need for support was widespread. MSA provided fifty-six grants to help sustain engagement and service delivery.

"When you run an organization that is based on people serving in person and no one can do anything in person, that's as disruptive as you can get," explains MSA's CEO, Emily Haber. "As a state service commission, we could see what was needed. The nonprofit community, especially small nonprofits, was struggling and, thanks to these funds, are now in better shape to engage volunteers."

MSA's Host Sites Sustained Members

Through MSA's financial support and technical assistance, nearly all the host sites in Massachusetts were able to keep their service members. Moreover, through training, mini grants, and, of course, service members themselves, Massachusetts Service Alliance successfully shored up the nonprofit infrastructure, enabling the continuity of operations amid the most disruptive event affecting nonprofits in history.

Lessons for the Long Term

With all its disruption, COVID-19 did not change the impact potential of national and state service in any of its three primary arenas—benefiting communities, developing service members, and strengthening the talent pipeline. Nevertheless, it has accelerated conversations about how we consider and integrate those impacts. While the lessons are still unfolding, some takeaways are already evident:

- Recent crises dramatically expanded how leaders think about the potential of service, seeing greater adaptability, responsiveness, and expeditiousness.
- Prioritizing equity in recruiting is critical but insufficient to create a more diverse corps. Meaningful advances in equity require meaningful changes to standard operating procedures.
- Innovation is an iterative process. Ongoing evaluation and adaptation are the only ways to ensure that an initiative achieves the intended impacts.
- Partnerships bring together unique skills and assets. Though at times challenging, when built on shared goals and deep commitment to finding solutions, public-private partnerships have the potential to address not only urgent crises, but also ongoing community needs.
- Strengthening the nonprofit and public sector through a skilled, experienced workforce is not just an investment in the future. New circumstances, at times, demand new practices in the *present.* Consequently, investing in equipping current staff with skills, support,

and resources is vital to ensuring organizational continuity and sustainability.

- With every engagement, consider how engaging volunteers benefits the clients, how service enriches the lives of the volunteers, and how training and supporting a skilled volunteer workforce enhances the nonprofit sector through talent development. While considering all three impact goals in the planning and evaluation can help organizations more fully optimize service and maximize impact, remember to note whether any impact goals compete with others and prioritize them accordingly. In this way, all organizations can benefit from looking at impacts through a multifaceted lens.

Disruption Exposed Our Lack of Infrastructure; It's Time to Build It

Craig Young

Craig Young is President of the Craig Young Family Foundation and Board Chair/Volunteer Executive Director of Inspiring Service. He serves on numerous other nonprofit boards with annual budgets ranging from modest to nearly three billion dollars. He also serves on the National Alliance for Volunteer Engagement and Encore Network leadership teams. Technology companies he founded in the 1980s and 1990s were later sold to Siemens and Apple. Over the last two decades, Craig has parlayed his business success into tangible social impact through a variety of efforts by leveraging his continued interest in technology into creating solutions for what he sees as inane absurdities holding back the independent sector.

* * *

Throughout the 1970s and 1980s, many late-night newscasts opened with the question: "It's 11:00 p.m., do you know where your children are?" The clear implication was that if you didn't know, little good—and quite possibly a good deal of bad—could happen.

Because almost no one in America knew where their community's "active" nonprofits were in 2020, "bad" is exactly what happened for many of them in communities across the country as the disruption of the pandemic hit and was followed by social reckoning. Disruption of services, furloughs, and closures resulted from having no way to share how they were being affected and what they needed now with the many who wanted to help.

"Active" nonprofits are 501c3 organizations and their fiscally sponsored programs that actively provide services to make life better for a community beyond their own members. They usually engage volunteers beyond just their board of trustees to deliver on their missions.

The 10 Percent Improvement Approach

In 2020, only a handful of cities and only one state could reasonably answer "yes" to the question, "Do you know where your active nonprofits are?" Sure, the local community foundation, United Way, and similar organizations know which nonprofits they are funding and some of the nonprofits they have declined. Volunteer centers and some associations know the subset of nonprofits they work with on a regular basis.

But talking with leaders of all these organizations, in many communities, reveals that more than half and as much as three-quarters of the active nonprofits in their own communities are unknown even to them. And the ones they *do* know are more likely to be larger, better funded, and white-led. Many of the often unseen and lesser-known nonprofits are led by people of color and women. And if we don't know where these nonprofits are, we can't know how they are doing or what they need. This perpetuates the gross inequities and imbalances surrounding how communities support their nonprofits.

You might think the Internal Revenue Service (IRS) database or services based on that database such as Guidestar, Pro Publica, and others reveal which are the active nonprofits. Unfortunately, they do not and there are several reasons why. Most, if not all, of the information provided by those services comes from each organization's 990 tax return after it is reviewed by the IRS. Small, active nonprofits with under fifty thousand dollars in revenue are not required to file a return and often go unnoticed. The information of fiscally sponsored organizations, who can be very active, is consolidated with that of their fiscal sponsor and goes unseen. And all of the information based on tax returns is out of date because it is not available until at least six to ten months after the end of the year being reported. In September of 2021, for example, the latest information you could see for most organizations was from 2019, which was before the start of the impact of the pandemic.

Even when the 990 information becomes available, it provides very little insight into what the organization does, how it does it, how to contact them, or what it might need. And the vast majority (estimated to be as much as 95 percent) of the

501c3 organizations in good standing in the IRS database are not actually active in helping their community with services beyond their own members or making charitable contributions. Moreover, the IRS website states that over ninety-five thousand new organizations apply for 501c3 status every year. Their initial tax information will likely not be seen for nearly two years. So, unless you already know the name or Employee Identification Number (EIN) of an organization that has been operating for a while, looking for information from these services is like looking for a needle in a haystack.

So, does being able to easily find, learn about, and connect with the active nonprofits in your community or state really matter? Could it significantly increase community engagement and therefore impact? Could it help save vital organizations during an emergency? The answer to all three of those questions is, "Yes, yes, and yes."

To be clear, many active nonprofits have survived in their communities without a sophisticated GPS-like navigational system to find them. They gain volunteers and donors from the "inside-out," with an occasional outsider being persistent enough to find them and connect with them. Long before the arrival of the internet and social media, support for organizations grew by the word of mouth of its current supporters. This continues to be a major source of new supporters with "word of mouth" now extended through social media.

But as we have become a far more mobile society, and as the nonprofit landscape continues to change at a much faster pace, when inspired, many more people are seeking to find their place or find their way to help on their own. Unfortunately, if they do not find something quickly and easily, they go back to their normal lives, and a potential supporter is lost. The marginally effective platforms operating in most cities and states today only measure the few successes—and not the many failures—to make a connection. So, where many nonprofits survive thanks to word of mouth, many others do not. We need platforms that are at least ten times more effective at making quality connections that could result in ten times or more the support. And by revealing the good work and the needs of the lesser known and often unseen nonprofits, we can reduce the inequity built into the current support systems.

The Ten Times Better Principle

In the field of innovation, it is widely understood that if you want to improve something by 10 percent, you can probably do it by tweaking the current approach or technology. But if you want to improve something by ten times or more, you need a fresh, innovative approach or technology. For example, paper maps provided an effective means to navigate and chart directions for many centuries. But it was not until we had GPS technology that getting directions became ten times (10X) or even one hundred times easier and more efficient. This increase in efficiency was only possible because of a significant investment in the satellite infrastructure for GPS technology which spurred follow-on investments in navigation devices, software, and smartphones. But it is not just about efficiency; think about how many lives have been saved because people or animals could be located with GPS.

As president of a family foundation for over twenty-five years, I—along with my fellow trustees—have always preferred organizations that leverage the value of engaging volunteers skillfully and thoughtfully. The assets in our family foundation were the result of my success starting and building software technology companies providing products to companies like Apple Computer in the 1980s and 1990s. From the beginning, we carefully considered the contribution that volunteers made to an organization. After over a decade of providing grants, serving on boards, and working with youth in a variety of capacities, we started investing time and money in technology-based nonprofits to make it easier and more equitable for youth to volunteer.

We got a few things right and a few things wrong, but most importantly we realized the approach we took was the 10 percent improvement approach. Like so many before and after us, we based our efforts on what we now refer to as a "post and hope" approach. Seeing the earlier success of dating platforms like match.com, everyone assumed that volunteers and donors would successfully connect in a similar way. With our investments and experiences, we thought we would provide a better user experience and make it more attractive (i.e., 10 percent better), which would yield great results. But we only saw modest improvements.

"Post and Hope" Approach Doesn't Work

As it turns out, the desire to help nonprofits is different from the desire to find a mate after all! When people want to meet someone new, they generally want to do it quickly—today, tomorrow, or sometime this week. If it doesn't happen right away, they are still interested next week, next month, and even next year. However, when someone becomes inspired to find a place or find a way to help in their community, and that "place" or "way" is not found fairly quickly, the inspiration soon fades. Put simply, a "connection" must be made quickly and easily; timing is important. The "post and hope" approach requires getting the timing right for both parties. The nonprofit hopes that someone interested in their cause sees and responds to their request for a volunteer on Tuesday at 4:00 p.m.—in time to meet their need. If they repeatedly post and no one responds, they stop posting, and when a potentially interested person finally does come, they find nothing.

To understand the importance of creating a connection quickly and easily, we need to look at what tends to "spark" a desire within a person to help a cause or community in the first place. If you haven't been thinking about helping any day for the last month, odds are you won't think about it today unless something happens to spark or inspire your desire to help. We see these sparks falling into one of three categories: a national or international event such as the 9/11 attacks, a community tragedy such as a four-year-old foster care child being found dead in a local park, or a personal event such as a family member stricken by a disease. This "spark," then, is what ignites that person to want to reach out to help, and it usually touches them in a deeply personal way. It is very rare that someone just decides "it's time to help" out of the blue.

Beginning in 2017, our family foundation began investing in technology aimed at providing tenfold (10X) improvement in a community's nonprofit infrastructure. The goal was to create comprehensive, easy-to-use guides (like Yelp provides for finding where to eat) based on modern technology and user experience. When you are in an unfamiliar neighborhood, for instance, and you want Thai for dinner, Yelp will make you aware of all of your options so you can make a more well-informed decision about which Thai restaurant to choose! As we saw much success in the communities we supported and several others where we later learned they were taking a similar approach, the question became: Why has this only happened in a handful of cities?

The answer is simple: because this is hard and it takes real work. Technologists love to build platforms and hand them off to others to fill with content; it's easy, it's fast, and it's fun. The problem is that in this case, it doesn't work. You assume that if you invite all nonprofits to complete a profile that could attract volunteers and donations, they will do it because it is in their best interest. Over and over, however, we have seen that this just doesn't happen.

For example, recently in a metro area with a population of over two million with about one thousand active nonprofits, these organizations were invited to build simple profiles for a giving campaign that included significant prizes and wide publicity and promotion. Fewer than one hundred of those nonprofits built a profile, and only a couple dozen actually participated. Nonprofits are notoriously under resourced, overworked, and often not particularly tech-savvy. They are highly focused on delivering on their missions, so they are only likely to invest effort when they believe there is a high probability of a quick return.

In the places that have useful, comprehensive guides, someone *outside* of the nonprofits builds the profiles for or with the nonprofits to ensure that these guides are thorough and consistent. This is hard to do for several reasons. First, it is hard to identify who are the active nonprofits in a community. We have seen across the country that even in modest-sized (population over fifty thousand) communities there is rarely anyone who has a complete, up-to-date list of the active nonprofits. The information for a profile often needs to be compiled from a variety of sources, including their website (which is often antiquated and out of date), tax records, social media accounts, and by contacting them directly to seek to find the right person. Yes, the return on investment is high—generally less than the value of one volunteer or donation—but the work is hard. Although much of the information in a profile is "evergreen," it is still important to maintain the accuracy of the information in the guide because mission statements, websites, contacts, volunteer programs, and other important information can change. Plus, new nonprofits often become active, old nonprofits close, and some nonprofits merge with another nonprofit.

Nonprofit Guide Impact Vast and Promising

In the same way that GPS data opened previously unimagined applications like Yelp, Airbnb, Uber, and more, the impact possible from potential applications that leverage a well-maintained, comprehensive active nonprofit guide are vast and promising.

Beyond mission delivery volunteering and donations, a guide could provide the foundation for collecting data in an emergency situation like a pandemic, finding board candidates and individual or teams of skilled volunteers, and other yet-to-be imagined applications. But just like all the GPS-based applications, an investment in infrastructure needs to be made to unlock and realize all this potential.

Most volunteering is done and donations are made at the local level, so people in communities tend to be attracted to local platforms because they assume they will be more complete and up to date. Back in the 1970s and 1980s, the Yellow Pages were the means of finding local businesses. Yet, today, people use worldwide applications like Yelp and Uber for their local needs because they have become more complete and up-to-date than local services. But Yelp and Uber didn't start as worldwide services, they were initially built out to be complete in selected communities like San Francisco and New York. We have invested in bringing nonprofit guides to a variety of communities of all sizes across the country, and we have come to learn that this work can best be done first at the state level and consolidated up to the national level and shared down to the local level.

Some States are Putting Better Infrastructure in Place

The good news is that in response to the disruptions of 2020, several more states—through their state community service commissions—have come to understand how they can have greater impact through better infrastructure. This is important because states and their residents need to have access to quality information and be able to find ways to engage with, support, and connect with their active nonprofits. State community service commissions have a federally funded and mandated mission to improve lives, strengthen communities, and foster civic engagement through service and volunteering. This is the way we can make it ten times easier to help and have ten times the impact we have today. Think about how many nonprofits we could have saved in 2020 if we would have only known where they were and what they needed.

Fast forward into the future. Imagine asking anyone the question, "Do you know where your active nonprofits are?"

With hard work, planning, collaboration, and by using the "ten times better (10X)" principle, the answer to that question can be, "Yes."

"Yes, I *do* know. And I know they are safe and sound."

About the Editors

Doug Bolton is a trained journalist with experience in print, broadcast, digital, and all forms of media. He spent thirty years in the media business, including nearly fifteen years as a business journal publisher. In 2011, he was recruited to run a geographic division of what is now the world's second largest commercial real estate services firm. Community nonprofit leadership roles led Doug to begin working in 2018 with Inspiring Service founders Craig and Michael Young on deploying technology and services to more efficiently and effectively build volunteer ecosystem infrastructure for hands-on service to board-level leadership.

As president of VQ Volunteer Strategies, **Beth Steinhorn** partners with organizations and their leadership to increase impact through strategic and innovative volunteer engagement. Beth has authored multiple books and articles on strategic volunteer engagement and helped found The National Alliance for Volunteer Engagement to advance the national dialogue about volunteerism and engagement. Prior to becoming a consultant, Beth worked as an executive director and marketing director with education and faith-based organizations and spent years working with museums as an educator, manager, and anthropologist. She draws upon her anthropology experience still, helping organizations shift their culture to embrace volunteer engagement as a strategy to fulfill mission.

Jerome Tennille is a Corporate Responsibility and Social Impact strategist who works in the hospitality industry and advises on volunteerism independently. His work focuses on designing, planning, and executing corporate employee volunteer programming to create positive social and environmental impact. He has expertise in bringing corporations and nonprofits together to build strategies that help advance long-term community goals and drive employee engagement. Prior to his work in corporate responsibility, he was the Senior Manager of Volunteer Services for Tragedy Assistance Program for Survivors (TAPS), a national nonprofit that serves military families experiencing loss. Jerome is also a social impact writer, and his work has been featured on Impakter, Business 2 Community Magazine, VolunteerMatch, Nonprofit Information.com and many other outlets. Jerome holds a Master of Sustainability Leadership from Arizona State University and is designated as Certified in Volunteer Administration (CVA). Jerome is also a veteran of the U.S. Navy.

Craig Young is President of the Craig Young Family Foundation and Board Chair/Volunteer Executive Director of Inspiring Service. He serves on numerous other nonprofit boards with annual budgets ranging from modest to nearly three billion dollars. He also serves on the National Alliance for Volunteer Engagement and Encore Network Leadership Teams. Technology companies he founded in the 1980s and 1990s were later sold to Siemens and Apple. Over the last two decades, Craig has parlayed his business success into tangible social impact through a variety of efforts by leveraging his continued interest in technology into creating solutions for what he sees as inane absurdities holding back the independent sector.